The globalization of the western cultural revolution

KEY CONCEPTS, OPERATIONAL MECHANISMS

Translated from the French by Benedict Kobus

Marguerite A. Peeters
Updated Third English Edition
Copyright 2023

⚓ENROUTE
Make the time

En Route Books and Media, LLC
5705 Rhodes Avenue
St. Louis, MO 63109

Contact us at contact@enroutebooksandmedia.com

ISBN-13: 979-8-88870-046-4
Library of Congress Control Number: 2023938447

Front cover painting:
"Mary on her return from visiting Elizabeth" Paul L. Peeters
Copyright on Front Cover Image © 2023 by John P. Peeters

Back cover painting:
"Master, where do you live?" Paul L. Peeters

CONTENTS

ABBREVIATIONS

CEDAW	Convention on the Elimination of All Forms of Discrimination against Women
CLADEM	Committee for the Defense of the Rights of Women in Latin American and the Carribeans
DAW	Division for the Advancement of Women
ECOSOC	Economic and Social Council
ILO	International Labor Organization
INSTRAW	UN International Research and Training Institute for the Advancement of Women
IPPF	International Planned Parenthood Federation
IUSSP	International Union for the Scientific Study of Population
MDG	Millennium Development Goals
NATO	North Atlantic Treaty Organisation
NEPAD	New Partnership for Africa's Development
NGO	Non-governmental organization
OECD	Organisation for Economic Co-operation and Development
UN	United Nations
UNAIDS	UN AIDs Program
UNDP	UN Development Program
UNESCO	Agence de l'ONU pour l'Education et la Culture
UNICEF	UN Fund for Children
UNIFEM	UN Women's Fund
UNFPA	UN Fund for Population Activities
WEDO	Women's Environment and Development Organization
WHO	World Health Organization

Preface to the 2023 edition

Living in Western Ukraine between 1991 and 1993, I was an eye-witness of the downfall of the Soviet Empire. I shall never forget the historic hope in people's hearts to rebuild their country according to universal human aspirations: freedom, and in particular religious freedom and the freedom to determine themselves according to their history and cultural identity, peace, respect for the family as the fundamental cell of society, East-West solidarity, fraternity and friendly cooperation. An unexpected challenge soon compromised those noble aspirations. In 1994, a member of the Holy See delegation to the UN's Fourth International Conference on Population (Cairo) opened my eyes to a new threat for humanity. The International Planned Parenthood Federation and like-minded pressure groups aggressively sought to globally impose new "norms" incorporating the neo-Marxist or postmodern objectives of the Western sexual and feminist revolution, such as *sexual and reproductive health* and *gender*. Marxism-Leninism had imploded, but emerging global governance was installing operational mechanisms to spread the Western cultural revolution and its foremost byproduct – rapid and profound secularization – to all corners of the world.

I participated as a journalist in all the UN conferences that followed Cairo. The UN had launched a series of nine post-Cold War conferences to build a "new global consensus" for the 21st century. I immediately understood that what was at stake went far beyond sexual morality issues. A new global language, absent from the UN's foundational documents and forged by "experts", was then becoming the object of this "global consensus". It covered all the domains of international cooperation: socioeconomic, environmental, human rights, political, ethical, anthropological, cultural and even religious. It spread like wildfire no sooner was the conference process over. A new synthesis was emerging, vastly differing from that on which the UN had been founded in 1945. History was then in the making. The new world vision did largely win the day. To significant extents, it has governed us since the mid-1990s.

In 2003, I was invited to address the plenary assembly of the Regional Episcopal Conference of Western Africa. It was the first in a series of missions to the continent. The 150 bishops present directly connected my description of global governance's agendas and strategies with the concrete challenges they were confronted with on their pastoral ground. They wanted to grasp the mechanisms of the neo-colonization they were painfully experiencing. They asked me to write a sort of manual that would didactically expose the history and development of the globalization of the Western sexual and feminist revolution. The book came out in 2007, and African episcopal conferences distributed it to bishops, formation centers and seminaries. Interest about these issues arose in the West and other parts of the world when the gender agenda started becoming a more visible reality in education reform, culture and laws. This book was then republished in a number of countries. It reached five continents.

In my PhD thesis, I distinguished three great periods in the global governance revolution. The seminal and gestational stage unfolded in the shade of the Cold War (1945-89). The revolution itself took place during the UN's post-Cold War international conferences (1990-96). Ever since the last of these conferences, the process entered its implementation stage (1996 to present). Two successive normative frameworks for international cooperation characterize this implementation stage: the Millennium Development Goals (2000-2015), and Agenda 2030, including the Sustainable Development Goals (2015-2030).

This book is a republication of the second, 2012 edition to which I only brought minor adjustments. It covers the first two stages and part of the third stage of the global governance process. It does not address Agenda 2030. I did not deem it necessary to update it, as its primary purpose is to provide an overview of the history of the global agenda now governing us. In my analysis, Agenda 2030 only consolidates the vision set during the revolution. It uses the novel language then coined. It rests on the same conceptual pillars. It is driven by the same ideological objectives.

Introduction

The practical purpose of this *manual* is to provide educators in developing countries with the information they need in order to gain, in the light of eternal law written by God himself in the hearts of all people, knowledge and discernment of the key concepts and operational mechanisms that make up the globalization of the western cultural revolution.

By *global cultural revolution* we mean the dissemination throughout the world, since the end of the cold war, of a new ethic: secularist in its radical dimensions, this ethic is the outcome of the twentieth century's feminist, sexual and cultural revolutions and of the long course taken by the West towards postmodernity.

This manual does not attempt to exhaust the subject. It concentrates on analyzing those historical developments which we deem the most pertinent in revealing the strong cultural tendencies of the revolution.

The global cultural revolution embraces all aspects of life in society. This manual particularly focuses on the study of the anthropological challenges involved in the globalization of the western *feminist* and *sexual* revolutions. We believe that the deconstruction of Judeo-Christian anthropology is at the source of the socio-political dysfunctions which mark today's world governance.

In view of its didactic purpose, this manual has few references. However, the matter it contains comes from very numerous sources as well as from a wide variety of personal contacts. The author's chief source is the interviews she conducted with leading global governance experts and agents at the major international conferences of the United Nations since that of Cairo in 1994. Since 1995, she has published more than 310 analytical reports (over 3,000 pages) on multilateral developments in the framework of *Interactive Information Services* (IIS). IIS reports refer directly to documents and texts sourced from international organizations.

One might think that the developments analyzed in this manual are widely known, particularly by heads and decision-makers in education, health and politics. In fact, there is still abyssal ignorance about the anthropological challenges of the revolution and the new ethic.

Ignorance leads to a generalized apathy, or even indifference, with serious consequences for the future of humanity.

The challenges are complex. This manual aims to promote the kind of discernment which can only be obtained by dint of effort. Discernment does not mean uprooting the tares growing alongside the good wheat, but learning to recognize them and to harvest the good wheat. Once the distinction has been perceived, the way is opened for a new advance, a new leadership able to respond in a positive and hopeful way to the genuine aspirations of humanity at the beginning of the third millennium.

In the West, the revolution is achieving its chief objectives and even seems to have reached the point of self-destruction. For a generation, the battlefront has moved to developing countries, particularly Africa, and to Central and Eastern European nations. This manual is destined primarily to our friends in the non-Western world, whom we wish to encourage to be faithful to who they are and, by remaining themselves, to offer today's world a leadership which is specific to them and is already awaited by those who, all over the world, are yearning for a return to reality, truth and love.

THE WESTERN FEMINIST, SEXUAL AND CULTURAL REVOLUTION

The feminist and sexual revolution of the last century has achieved most of its objectives in the West. Its propositions, outlawed at the beginning of the 20th century, now impregnate the fabric of western societies and are on course to becoming a global culture. Having overcome most bastions of political resistance, the revolution continues to spread its effects without meeting any cultural resistance. Western civilization is now tasting its bitter fruits and must confront its devastating existential consequences, while radicalism seems to have reached its peak.

This chapter introduces us to the history of the western feminist and sexual revolution and to the driving ideas of the individuals who have spearheaded it. It does not aim to be exhaustive, but to allow those who, on other continents, today suffer the full force of the effects of the revolution to grasp the real intentions of the social engineers and the often hidden radicalism of their objectives.

The West faced with the consequences of its revolution

In less than a century, the ideas of revolutionary minorities have deeply transformed the mentalities and mores of the majority in the West. The new culture not only accepts, permits and tolerates, but also "celebrates" the sexual experimentation of young people, the succession and multiplicity of partners, the diversity of "sexual orientations", and cohabitation outside marriage. For several generations, sexual education programmes in schools – not only public but also private – encourage promiscuity (if only implicitly, when they do not do so explicitly) and promote an ethic of free choice which bypasses the human and moral education of teenagers. The Internet and the rapid advances of technology put pornography within reach of an increasingly young and large audience. Have not a majority of young people, by the age of eighteen, experimented with everything and often even given up the hope and desire of starting a family? Increasingly coming from broken families, many of them no longer have the courage to commit themselves.

Most states in the West have decriminalized or legalized abortion and promulgated laws allowing artificial fertilization. Some allow genetic manipulation on surplus embryos for purely scientific, not reproductive, ends. Many of them, under the pressure of the powerful homosexual lobby which seems to be constantly gaining ground, have granted homosexual couples a juridical status comparable to marriage.

Homosexual proselytizing in schools, euthanasia (of fetuses as well as the seriously sick), legalization of sexual relations at lower and lower ages, so-called "surrogate mothers"[1], "homosexual parenting"[2], "therapeutic embryos"[3], "private eugenics"[4], research on embryos and embryonic stem cells, their financing and use in medicine are becoming a citizen's right. These aberrations no longer seem to shock mentalities, even when they accentuate an increasingly perceptible malaise in civilization.

The new culture claims the right to carry out all that is technically possible. This idea, with tragic consequences in western culture, goes back to Baruch Spinoza (1632 – 1677). It ends up in the practically insoluble dilemmas which now confront bioethics and goes as far as opening the door to cloning and "artificial wombs"[5]. Western culture is governed by an ethic known as *consensual*, but which is radically ambivalent and devoid of stable content. It has deconstructed conscience. Consequently, the majority can no longer distinguish good and evil. It has become easy to manipulate it: an unhealthy or even dangerous situation.

Having attacked the very structure of the human person, the revolution has provoked an anthropological cataclysm. Western culture shifted from the *family* to *couples* and *individuals*, from *spouses* to *partners*, from *marriage* to *free love*, from *happiness* to *well-being* and *quality of life*, from *parental authority* to *children's rights*, from *self-giving* to *ownnership of one's body* and *control over one's destiny*, from *conscience* to *free choice*, from interpersonal *communion* to the *fusion* of nameless and faceless individuals, from *complementarity of man and woman* to a *contract between the sexes*, from *parents* to *reproducers*, from *procreation* to *reproduction*, from all forms of *legitimate authority* to individuals' *empowerment* and *experimentation*.

The culture of *ownership*, *power* and *pleasure* that the revolution sought to create has not brought about the expected liberation. Revolutionary radicalism is now confronted by the failure of its utopian project. No one can any longer deny the existential and socioeconomic consequences of conjugal infidelity, divorce, abortion, euthanasia, the contraceptive mentality, *in vitro* fertilization, and the trivialization of the "morning after pill". These practices, which have become common currency, wound those who commit them as well as to those on whom they are carried out or those who witness them. The consequences of the cultural revolution are before us: fragmentation in the family, in society and between generations, loneliness and abandonment of the elderly, emotional troubles and suffering of children living in "single parent" or "reconstituted" families, increase in cases of depression, anthropological deconstruction, academic failures, professional disorientation, increase in suicides, despair and feelings of insecurity in young people who then seek refuge in drugs, violence, sects and satanism, loss of cultural traditions and faith. The extent of these dysfunctions has become so great that they have a destructuring effect on society as a whole. Paradoxically, deconstruction has already become *systemic*.

It is becoming apparent to the majority that the system put in place by the revolution is not sustainable and that it is not unrelated to what is in fact a breakdown of the international order. Are not the current difficulties in satisfactorily reforming the multilateral system explained by the lack of will to address the roots of the problem?

Nevertheless the social engineers, belatedly, continue to deny the real causes of the current state of western societies and to look for alibis. They perpetuate and aggravate the harm by applying false remedies. They even think that they are more necessary than ever to resolve the problems that they themselves have contributed to creating: the high occurrence of sexually transmitted diseases and AIDS, violence against women, single mothers, the increase of what they call "unwanted pregnancies" and "unsafe" abortions and so on. Backed up by networks of global partners with vested interests, the agents of social change remain powerful.

Political leaders prove unable to take advantage of the self-destruction of the revolution's perverse objectives in order to propose a positive and sustainable alternative. Their absence of moral leadership abandons the multitude to themselves. A vague and spontaneous desire to return to common sense, happiness and stability is seen mainly in young people, but this desire is seldom satisfied since their elders are unable to offer them the guidance they seek.

The end of myths

In spite of their activism, the militants, whom we will identify more specifically in the course of the following chapters, have lost their doctrinaire momentum. At the end of its course, the revolution produces no new concepts, no more "grand theories", no more global ideologies[6]. The myths on which the revolution was founded have quietly fallen by themselves, one after the other.

- The *myth of overpopulation* forged by Malthus[7] sustained the western population control movement and demographic policies for a century and a half. The myth no longer stands up to reality. The signs of a "demographic winter" are there: a dramatic lowering of fertility rates and population growth, inverted demographic pyramids, birth rates below replacement level, inexorable aging of the population. The crisis is bringing, particularly in Europe, social fragmentation, unmanageable increases in public spending, depletion of state coffers, economic recession, growing poverty among pensioners. The West's capacity to exercise its responsibility to the world is diminished. Many talk of the *end of the West* – a development not without global consequences.

- The *myth of women's liberation* and of *male oppression* no longer attracts young people. The militant feminist movement, now represented by a generation in their sixties, which is no longer being renewed, has, besides, been retreating on some of its positions for the last twenty years. More recently, a current of thought in the United States has been seeking to deconstruct what Warren Farrell called "*the myth of male power*"[8] and to show how much feminist hysteria has exploited it.

- The *myth of "free love"* is falling apart before the devastated landscape of a society of broken families, unwed and divorced people, children and young people with no parents and no reference point, the proliferation of sexually transmitted diseases and AIDS, and the incontrovertible psychological consequences of abortion. If many young people, left to themselves by the generations who made the revolution, continue to wander aimlessly, they are disillusioned and no longer adhere to the doctrine of the myth. They discover by bitter experience that "free love" is not the way of lasting happiness. The exaltation given by the abolition of taboos and the illusory feeling of power is ephemeral and rapidly gives way to disenchantment.

- The *myth of progress* has now been replaced by an obsession with sustainability and a culture of fear geared towards "zero growth". Changing our lifestyles to ensure the survival of humanity and of the planet has become a priority in education. *Hedonistic consumerism* is practical but no longer doctrinaire.

- Finally, the *myth of scientific autonomy* and the *absolutization of "scientific certitudes"* has also crumbled. Psychology and sociology in particular, have given up clearly identifying the "laws" of human behavior as they strove to do before. Freud's psychoanalysis and his dogma on the libido are losing ground. The fraud of the so-called "sexology" at the origin of sex education programs used for the last fifty years in the West has recently been discredited, as we shall see later in this chapter.

The collapse of myths used by the revolution does not prevent powerful industries, with huge financial stakes, from sustaining deconstruction in the West and propagating it elsewhere in the world: the film industry, above all the music industry, the media, advertising, pornography, abortion, contraceptives[9] and condoms, nightclubs, prostitution, fashion and drugs. Their propaganda uses increasingly effective and sophisticated technical and operational means to condition and transform mentalities.

In reality, the true battlefront has now moved to developing countries, where human and cultural values and traditions tend to prove more resilient and are not yet fully aligned with the new ethic. The so-called countries in transition (formerly communist) and newly created states have also provided new territories for the spreading of the revolution, which has wasted no time in occupying them rapidly. Finally, as we shall see in chapter six, the monotheistic religions represent the last line of attack of the revolution. The agents of social change seek, in ways that have become more evident in the last few years, to penetrate *within* religions so as to change their teachings as well as the behavior of believers. In the final analysis, is not a new global ethic, no longer effectively opposed by any influential social actor, imposing itself *de facto*?

The feminist revolution and the beginnings of the sexual revolution in the West

To gain a better grasp of the ideological issues of the global cultural revolution of the 1990s, which we shall analyze in the following chapters, let us take a bird's-eye view of the well-known course of the western feminist and sexual revolution in the twentieth century.

The feminist revolution, the sexual revolution and the cultural revolution are historically distinct phenomena. In their radical content, however, these three revolutions became increasingly integrated in the course of the twentieth century. The feminist revolution came first. Its first wave goes back to the nineteenth century[10]. At the beginning of the twentieth century, a certain feminist current began to claim access to contraceptive methods, abortion and sexual freedom: it was setting the foundations for the sexual revolution. The sexual revolution burst into full development in the 1960s, partly merging with the second wave of the feminist movement and bringing about the cultural revolution of May 1968. Today the tidal wave of the western cultural revolution has reached every shore and is spreading its effects throughout the world.

At the beginning of the nineteenth century women did not enjoy the right to vote or to own property and were excluded from public office and higher education. Napoleon's legislation and the French civil code promulgated in 1804 gave man a higher status and consequently excluded women from certain social and political activities. The industrial revolution separated domestic life from economic life, spheres which were previously integrated. This separation had particularly negative social consequences for women and poor mothers. Historically, the feminist movement was born to react against the social and juridical marginalization of women. At the outset, the movement was organized mainly in France, England and the United States.

The first women's rights congress was held in Seneca Falls (New York, USA) in 1848. The Seneca Falls declaration claimed the complete equality of women before the law, their right of access to education and to economic power, their right to equal pay for equal work, and their right to vote. A feminist congress later took place in Paris in 1878.

The suffragette movement, which sometimes had recourse to violence, developed at the turn of the century. Several countries granted women the right to vote at the beginning of the twentieth century. Feminism then set off in new directions. It began to fight for socioeconomic parity and access by women to jobs traditionally reserved for men. Access to contraception and abortion became for the majority of feminists the condition of respect for women's rights.

The feminist movement rapidly became radicalized in different ways according to ideologies, becoming a struggle against the social order and its values, the family and marriage, considered as forms of oppression against women.

In the United States, Margaret Sanger (1879 - 1966)[11] and Emma Goldman (1869 - 1940)[12] launched anti-conception and abortion campaigns and began to speak of single women's sexuality (lesbianism). In England, Marie Stopes (1880 - 1958)[13], a disciple of Sanger, worked in the same direction. Sanger opened the first American birth control clinic in Brooklyn in 1916. Stopes opened a birth control clinic in London in 1921. At the time the Malthusian antinatalist leagues were particularly active in Europe. Their objectives reinforced the feminist claims.

In 1920 the precursors of the sexual revolution already formed a small but very aggressive international network. It held a congress in London in 1929 and founded the *World League for Sexual Reform*. Karl Marx (1818 - 1883) and Friedrich Engels (1820 - 1895) considered that the "liberation of the woman" was part of the socialist revolution. A women's conference was held in Moscow in 1918. Under Lenin in the 1920s, the Soviet regime promoted the equality of women's rights.

The development of the contraceptive pill in the 1950s[14] gave the feminist and sexual revolutions the technical means to realize their subversive objectives. At first restricted to the family setting, contraception became increasingly used outside marriage. Very quickly after its commercialization at the beginning of the 1960s, the West experienced the revolt of young people, which reached its climax in May 1968. Legalization of abortion was not long in following: 1973 in the United States (Supreme Court *Roe vs. Wade* ruling), and 1975 in France. With the right to abortion, feminists deemed that they had acquired definitive control over their sexuality. In the 1960s feminism became a political force in the United States.

A complex phenomenon

Feminism is one of the major sociopolitical movements of the last two centuries. It is a complex phenomenon. At the outset and still today in situations of objectively unacceptable injustice, particularly in developing countries, feminism has sought to promote and defend the human dignity of women and their right to be treated in an equal way by the law. However, an individualistic and dialectical conception of the relation between men and women[15] corrupted from the start the different ways in which the movement interpreted the concepts of equality and identity in the West.

In the course of its history, feminism has surfed on different ideological waves, of which here are a few examples:

- *Egalitarianism*: making women equal in everything to men in terms of social roles, with the consequent deconstruction of the anthropological difference between the sexes.

- *Dualism*: this type of feminism recognizes, to a certain extent, feminine specificity but it creates a dialectical opposition between man and woman.

- *Liberalism*: liberal feminists have sought to monopolize sociopolitical and economic power while giving it an absolute value.

- *Marxism, socialism*: socialist feminists have led a "war of the sexes" to "liberate" the woman from masculine "oppression" through their work and their acquisition of economic power.

- *Eco-feminism*: eco-feminists have integrated feminism and protection of *Gaia*, "Mother Earth"; they are generally in favor of demographic stabilization for ecological ends.

- *Freemasonry*: a Masonic feminist current first fought for the right of women to divorce and economic independence, then for their right to contraception, abortion and *in vitro* fertilization.

- *Protectionism*: these feminists concentrate on acquiring legal protections for women in the domain of work, divorce and freedom of expression.

- *Spiritualism*: witchcraft, *Dianic Wicca*, neo-pagan rites to *Hathor*, *Isis* and other goddesses, temples to "the Feminine", among others, belong to the practices of "spiritualist" feminists.

- *Postmodernity*: the prevailing postmodern feminist current postulates that everything is a social construct and denies that the words "man", "woman", "marriage" and "identity" have clear and stable meaning.

Feminism has also surfed on *anarchism, lesbianism, post-colonialism, existentialism, individualism, third-worldism...* The common objective of these diverse forms of feminism is to eradicate from culture the causes of feminine "inequality" and "oppression" and to restructure society from top to bottom according to their own ideological scheme - a scheme of deconstructing the established order and the order written in nature. The diversity of tendencies and the sometimes contradictory nature of their claims make of feminism an incoherent movement destined to self-destruction. In fact, do not some feminists themselves now speak of *post-feminism*?

Margaret Sanger and Simone de Beauvoir

Margaret Sanger is the figurehead of the feminist and sexual revolution. Her cultural influence and that of the *International Planned Parenthood Federation* (IPPF) which she founded[16], and her role in the moral deconstruction of the West are immeasurable. In this chapter it is necessary to pause, if briefly, to consider her thought and objectives in order to grasp the radicalism at the heart of current so-called *reproductive health* programs, which themselves have been at the center of population and development programs.

Sanger wanted to "liberate" the woman from what she called "the slavery of reproduction". According to her, the woman should be able to "own" her body and her sexuality. Being the "owner", she must be able to dispose of it as she wishes, to enjoy the "freedom of her body" and her "rights", and to "control her life". She said: "No woman can call herself free who does not own and control her body. No woman can call herself free until she can choose consciously whether she will or will not be a mother." Each child should henceforth be "wanted", "chosen", "planned", for according to Sanger, "a free race cannot be born of slave mothers"[17].

To acquire this "freedom", Sanger rebelled against the Church as much as against the State - against all that, according to her, "oppresses" the woman by maintaining control over her body as a "means of reproduction": the social institution of the family, civil, moral and religious law, dogmas, cultural traditions, conservative moralists, patriarchal systems, male domination, social and economic injustice, poverty, lack of education and information, lack of access to contraception[18] and abortion. The Catholic Church was for Sanger - herself of Irish Catholic stock - the greatest obstacle to the realization of her subversive objectives.

Sanger was a socialist. Her ideas were extended by Marxist feminists such as the American Shulamith Firestone (1945 -)[19], according to whom the fertility of the woman is the source of her oppression: Firestone concludes that we must fight "the oppressive power structures set up by nature and reinforced by man"[20]. Women must take control of the means of reproduction, just as the proletariat must take control of the means of production. Firestone wanted to demonstrate that feminism was the means of linking Marx with Freud. She wrote: "Freudianism has become, with its confessionals and penance, its proselytes and converts, with the millions spent on its upkeep, our modern Church". For Firestone, "The end goal of the feminist revolution is the elimination of the sex distinction itself"[21].

To carry out the revolution, feminists had to *grab power* - political power, social power, economic power, hence their cultural militancy and their radical politics. The revolution needed "brave and angry women", according to the world-renowned IPPF slogan.

To grab power, the sexual revolution linked its individualist objectives ("free love", pleasure-seeking, free rein given to the libido) to geopolitical ones. To promote contraception and abortion, its agents first invoked the *demographic* argument (overpopulation threatens the well-being and the survival of humanity), then the *environmental* argument (linking "overpopulation" with environmental degradation) and finally the *security* argument (AIDS, so-called "unsafe" abortion, and poverty are presented as threats to security on the individual as well as the global level). The international community has thus passed from *population control*[22], to *sustainable development* and finally to *human security*.

Arbitrary individual choice, or the *right to choose*, is the keystone of the new edifice. This concept has its source in the existentialism of

Simone de Beauvoir[23] (1908 - 1986) and Jean-Paul Sartre[24] (1905 - 1980). These intellectual leaders of atheistic existentialism wanted to make the individual exit ("ex-ist") from the conditions of existence as established by God so that he could be liberated from them, could choose "freely" and live for himself. To exercise his *right to choose*, the individual must, according to the logic of atheistic existentialism, engage in negating whatever exists outside himself - what is given by nature and divine Revelation. We would like to insist on this point: it is not a matter of passively denying reality and what is given, of not doing anything, but of active *commitment* in this negation. The refusal to commit morally thus contrasts with the demand for commitment in social activism.

Radical feminism belongs to this negation: "One is not born a woman, but becomes a woman," says Simone de Beauvoir in a formula that has been around the world. According to de Beauvoir, the being of a woman is not a "given" but a social construct. This construct may take many forms, depending on the attitude of the woman. If the woman remains passive and submits to traditions, she becomes a *spouse* and a *mother*: the "stereotype" or the "social construct" which feminists wish precisely to deconstruct, because they deem it repressive. If the woman engages in the construction of herself in a way which is radically autonomous vis-à-vis men, others and God, she "liberates" herself, becomes "herself" and lives for herself. She can thus *own herself* and *control her destiny*. From then on the existence of the woman is realized outside the designs of God, in a radically *autonomous* way.

The fraud of Alfred Kinsey and his "science" of sexuality

The biologist and zoologist, dubbed by his followers as the "father of sexology", Alfred Kinsey (1894 - 1956)[25] carried out studies on human sexuality, from the 1930s, at the University of Indiana in the United States. Kinsey professed the wish to establish the parameters of an "exact science" of sexuality. His real objective was to bring about a "sexual liberation" of society, a revolution to establish a *permissive society*. As a militant atheist, Kinsey wanted to thereby deconstruct western Judeo-Christian morality, which he represented as repressive.

His two publications, *Sexual Behavior in the Human Male* (a best-seller, published in 1948) and *Sexual Behavior in the Human Female* (1953) kicked off the western sexual revolution. Thus Kinsey has been one of the most influential people of our times. From the start of the 1950s pornography, which for him was "neutral" or "inoffensive", began to spread. His influence was exerted especially on sexual education programs used in the West since the 1960s. The homosexual movement has used his studies to give itself a "scientific" justification.

Kinsey presented himself as a "disinterested scientist". However, the alleged objectivity of his two reports has recently been discredited as a major scientific fraud[26]. To obtain his statistics, Kinsey relied on perverted volunteers, detained criminals, prostitutes, pimps, pedophiles, pederasts, homosexuals, rapists, sexual delinquents and predators, whom he classified as "normal" cases. "Normal" Americans for their part often refused to respond to his questionnaires.

Kinsey's radical atheism and his rejection of the person and of love led him to an *integral sexualization* of the human being - to a perverse and aberrant anthropological reductionism. He taught, for example, that children are led to the exercise of sexuality from their fourth month and that they have a *right* to it at all ages. He deemed it "vital" that they should exercise this "right" before the age of six, before being determined by cultural and religious "taboos". The personal destiny of man, his soul and spiritual values played for him no role.

For Kinsey, sexual liberation comes through the knowledge that the human being has of his "whole nature" thanks to science. The history of medicine proves, according to him, that man cannot make himself "free from bewildered fear, despondent shame, or arrant hypocrisy" unless he seek to "know himself and face his whole nature"[27]. But Kinsey approached *nature* through the lens of a *radical materialist naturalism*, and not as it is in reality.

Kinsey considers on the one hand that "The only unnatural sex act is that which you cannot perform"[28], and on the other that all sexual acts are good as long as they gratify the individual. In other words, for Kinsey all sexual acts, be they pedophilic, incestuous, homosexual, heterosexual, bisexual or still others, are "natural", and his logic implies that since these acts are "natural" they are "good". Witness to this belief is the following quotation from the actress Mae West (1893 - 1980): "If Kinsey is right, I have only done what comes naturally, what the average American does secretly, drenching himself in guilt fixations and phobias because of his sense of sinning. I have never felt myself a sinner or committed what I would call a sin."[29]

Kinsey refused to place people in categories according to what in today's language we would call "sexual orientation". For him, sexual liberation comes through the realization that "The living world is a continuum in each and every one of its aspects."[30]. The categories "homosexual – heterosexual" are for him fabrications of the human mind which must be deconstructed to arrive at "a sound understanding of the realities of sex"[31]. All sexual acts, whatever their nature, are inscribed on a *continuum*. Persons are "individuals who have had certain amounts of heterosexual experience and certain amounts of homosexual experience"[32]. Homosexuality, remarked Kinsey, was practiced in ancient Greece and is practiced today in numerous cultures where it is not taboo. He argues that this "fact" proves that the "capacity of an individual to respond erotically to any sort of stimulus, whether it is provided by another person of the same or opposite sex, is basic in the species."[33] Kinsey judged that the sexual behavior frameworks of an individual are determined either by experiences and habits or by the social pressures he receives.

Kinsey built a new ethic according to which moral and religious laws which imposed control of drives were contrary to "human dignity". The revolution he launched is largely responsible for abolishing the distinction between what is good and evil, between what is "normal" and what is "perverted" in western culture. Note that Kinsey's supposed "scientific authority" fooled the sixties generation, who by 1990 occupied the commanding positions in the globalization of the western sexual revolution.

Herbert Marcuse and the cultural revolution[34]

Herbert Marcuse (1898 - 1979) is the master of the western cultural revolution of the 1960s - a cultural revolution founded on eroticism, pleasure, *eros*. By turning them into culture, Marcuse transformed the powerful and growing waves of the feminist and sexual revolutions into a tidal wave.

In the preface of *Eros and Civilization*[35], Marcuse announced unequivocally that his purpose was social revolution. Like Freud (1856 - 1939), he believed that civilization was repressive and weakened drives by "civilizing" them. Recall the three divisions of the psyche according to Freud: the *id*, in other words the unconscious, which knows neither good nor bad, is free and fundamental; the *ego*, the mediator between the *id* and the outside world, which coordinates the *id*'s drives in order to minimize conflicts with reality (the *ego* is not at peace with itself: it has a defensive attitude, since reality is hostile); and the *superego*, namely the influence of parents, teachers, the state, institutions, laws and so on.

Marcuse advocated a cultural or erotic revolution to make civilization non-repressive. He wished to replace the system in place with a civilization allowing the individual to "be himself", freed from all social and institutional pressures. According to him, the new system should be formed and determined by those sexual drives themselves. Marcuse wanted to transform the instinctive needs of the individual into political values, the satisfaction of individual drives into a socially desirable objective. According to his ideology, the driving force of the revolution is not class struggle or economic development, but psychology, the psychological configuration of the individual, the nature of instincts. Marcuse synthesized Marx and Freud.

Freud defined human personality as a psycho-material substrate motivated by the quest for hedonistic gratification. Freudian psychoanalysis radicalized the principle according to which pleasure is the fundamental human drive: it reduced everything to libido. The fundamental error of Freud was to consider that reality contradicts pleasure, that it is its natural enemy and hence the enemy of humanity. One can grasp how western civilization has increasingly distanced itself from reality since Freudianism.

Marcuse adopted the nihilistic and Manichean vision which Freud had of culture. For Freud, civilization is based on the permanent subjugation of instincts, with repression and suffering as the result. The pessimism of Freud is fundamental: according to him, "happiness is no cultural value"[36], and "the history of man is the history of his repression"[37]. Marcuse goes further: the "destructive force" of instincts, he explains, "derives from the fact that they strive for a gratification which culture cannot grant: gratification as such and as an end in itself, at any moment"[38]. Instincts become human under the repressive influence of exterior reality - not that of nature but of man and society. Reality is thus a traumatizing experience, a force which opposes our aspirations. As for the unconscious, it keeps the objectives of the pleasure principle.

The principle of reality has been materialized into a system of institutions. Conscience, "the most cherished moral agency of the civilized individual, emerges as permeated with the death instinct; the categorical imperative that the superego enforces remains an imperative of self-destruction while it constructs the social existence of the personality."[39]

Is the suffering imposed by civilization on individuals worth the benefits of the culture which ensues? Marcuse says no. He would go on to formulate an alternative to repressive civilization - an objective which he considered achievable.

Marcuse defined freedom purely and simply as *absence of repression*. Freedom becomes an end in itself, a supreme value without content. Memory and imagination become the faculties of salvation: going back to the past and escaping reality through dream free us from repressive civilization. Marcuse spoke indeed of a "a compulsion inherent in organic life to restore an earlier state of things which the living entity has been obliged to abandon under the pressure of external disturbing forces"[40]. Regression would be the dominant tendency of human existence. The memory of the past is supposed to help us to rediscover ourselves. On the other hand, imagination is for Marcuse a form of mental activity which "retains a high degree of freedom from the reality principle even in the sphere of the developed consciousness"[41]. The activity of the imagination links the deepest levels of the unconscious to the highest productions of conscious activity; it connects dream and reality, and frees us, through dream, from repressive reality.

Marcuse also lauded sexual perversions. According to him, the child is not only unwanted but is also unnatural because it is opposed to instinct. The child is the living contradiction of pleasure; it is repressive because of the responsibility that it gives parents. Sexual perversions carry a greater promise of happiness than normal sexuality: "Claiming institutional freedom in a world of repression, they are often characterized by a strong rejection of that feeling of guilt which accompanies sexual repression."[42]

The western erotic revolution has deconstructed reality, nature, culture, civilization, tradition, authority, the rule of law, the image of the father, morality, religion, truth, good and evil, rationality, consciousness, objective knowledge, individual personality, personal happiness, eternal life, immortality, love of neighbor, friendship, affection.

It has replaced reality with sensual gratification, spiritual progress with regression, reason capable of discernment with the reasoning of denial, normal sexuality with perversions, spiritual love with narcissistic love, moral conscience with the unconscious, imagination and sensuality. As we shall see in the next chapter, the cultural fruits of deconstruction have been transformed into *global norms* during the global consensus-building process of the first half of the 1990s.

---

[1] Women who accept, often for financial gain, to bear the baby of another woman who is unable to have children.

[2] Adoption of children by homosexual couples.

[3] "Test-tube baby" killed so that its stem cells can be used for medical purposes.

[4] Genetic selection of embryos on the basis of their biological "quality".

[5] When children will be conceived *in vitro* and develop in an incubator until their "birth".

[6] What postmodernists call "meta-narratives".

[7] Thomas Robert Malthus (1766 - 1834), British economist, had developed theories according to which population growth threatened the well-being of humanity.

[8] Title of a work by Warren Farrell, published in 1993.

[9] The contraceptive pill is today the most frequently sold "medicine" in the world.

[10] During the Enlightenment, the first thrusts were seen in, among others, the thought of Lady Mary Wortley Montagu, that of the marquis de Condorcet (1743 - 1794), and in the work of Mary Wollstonecraft *A Vindication of the Rights of Women*, published in 1792. Certain historians of feminism go even further back, to the Middle Ages and to Christine de Pisan. It is also worth emphasizing the influence of British thinkers who played a decisive role in the intermediate period between the Enlightenment and the age of science (Auguste Comte): notably Jeremy Bentham, the father of utilitarianism (1748 - 1832), Thomas Robert Malthus (1766 - 1834), James Mill (1773 - 1836), John Stuart Mill (1806 - 1873) and Walter Bagehot (1826 - 1877).

[11] Margaret Sanger is the founder of the *International Planned Parenthood Federation* (IPPF). In 1914, in New-York, she launched the feminist monthly *The Woman Rebel* to promote birth control. She was imprisoned for publishing pornographic material. In 1921, she founded the *American Birth Control League* which in 1942 became the *Planned Parenthood Federation of America*. In 1922 she published *The Pivot of Civilization*. She died in 1966.

[12] Emma Goldman was an anarchist and nihilist. She accepted violence as a necessary evil in the process of social transformation.

[13] *Marie Stopes International*, founded in London in 1976, is today one of the principal institutions in the world promoting "sexual and reproductive health". Marie Stopes works in 39 countries on the five continents, and claims to provide information and services to some 4.3 million people.

[14] Encouraged by Margaret Sanger, Dr. Gregory Goodwin Pincus invented the contraceptive pill. He made the first trials on female rabbits, then from 1956 on Puerto Rican women.

[15] It is significant that the word *feminism* was coined by a utopian socialist thinker, Charles Fourier, in 1837. Fourier thought that the extension of women's rights was the principle of all social progress.

[16] The *International Planned Parenthood Federation*, a federation of family planning NGOs known by the abbreviation IPPF, was founded in Bombay in 1952 during a meeting of volunteers working for planning associations in eight countries. At the time, the world was hostile to the IPPF. The use and the sale of contraceptives was subject to police regulation.

[17] See womenshistory.about.com/library/qu/blqusang.htm.

[18] Access to contraception was for Sanger a question of "social justice".

[19] Firestone is the author of *The Dialectic of Sex - The Case for Feminist Revolution* (1979). Her thought is inspired by Freud, Marx, de Beauvoir and Engels.

[20] See seattle.wa.lwv.org/pubs/womhist2002.pdf.

[21] See en.wikiquote.org/wiki/shulamith_firestone.

[22] From 2.5 billion in 1950, global population rose to more than 6 billion in 2000. The international conferences on population had the objective of "demonstrating" the "dangers" of demographic growth, its "link" with the depletion of natural resources and growing poverty.

[23] In 1948 Simone de Beauvoir published *The Second Sex* and *The Ethics of Ambiguity*. In 1971, she joined the *Mouvement de Libération de la Femme*, which in France proposed sexual liberation, birth control and abortion. In their manifesto of 1971, 343 women admitted to having had abortions. Emma Goldman, Betty Friedan, Jane Fonda, Bella Abzug, Gloria Steinem, Kate Millett, and Susan Brownmiller are some examples of personalities who exerted a determining influence on the feminist movement.

[24] Jean-Paul Sartre (1905 - 1980) met Simone de Beauvoir in 1929. In 1943 he published his main philosophical work, *L'Etre et le Néant (Being and Nothingness)*.

[25] Born in a rigorist Methodist family, Kinsey came under the influence of the atheistic Darwinism prevalent at Harvard during his doctoral studies. In 1947 he founded the *Institute for Sex Research* at the University of Indiana, still active today under the title of the *Kinsey Institute*.

[26] In April 2004 a large group of American jurists (*American Legislative Exchange Council*) concluded that Kinsey's research contained fabricated statistics. In their book *The Kinsey Corruption: An Exposé on the Most Influential 'Scientist' of our Time*, Judith Reisman and Susan Brinkmann demonstrated the fraudulent quality of Kinsey's work. It relied, for example, on information provided by Rex King, a notorious rapist who had attacked more than 800 children. Though he was bisexual and pedophilic, Kinsey did everything to preserve his reputation - essential to his image as a "serious scientist" - as a married man.

[27] See en.wikiquote.org/wiki/Alfred_Kinsey.

[28] Ib.

[29] Ib.

[30] Ib.

[31] Ib.

[32] Ib.

[33] Ib.

[34] The analysis contained in this section on Marcuse comes from the study by Prof. Paul L. Peeters: "Herbert Marcuse: Eros and Civilization". 22 August 1974.

[35] Herbert Marcuse: Eros and Civilization. Vintage Edition. 1962.

[36] See www.marxists.org/reference/archive/marcuse/works/eros-civilisation/introduction.htm.

[37] Quoted by P. Peeters, p. 7.

[38] Herbert Marcuse: Eros and Civilization. Vintage Edition. 1962, p.11.

[39] Ib., p. 48.

[40] Ib., p. 22.

[41] Ib., p. 127.

[42] Ib., p. 45.

THE GLOBAL CULTURAL REVOLUTION, POSTMODERNITY AND THE NEW GLOBAL ETHIC

The western cultural revolution reached its peak and was achieving most of its objectives in the 1980s. It had solidly established its "gains" in politics and spread its effects to all aspects of social life in the West, particularly in the domain of education, by the time the cold war ended. Surfing on the wave of globalization, the western cultural revolution spread to the rest of the world at a vertiginous pace, thereby causing a *global cultural revolution* at the time when the international community was setting out to forge new norms to give an "ethical framework" to the new era which was opening up.

This chapter introduces us to the historical context in which the new ethic was built, its main challenges and the complex phenomenon of *postmodernity*, the dominant feature of this ethic. It also shows the causal relation between the western cultural revolution and postmodernity.

The international conjuncture in 1989

The fall of the Berlin Wall in 1989 marked the entry into a new era for humanity. The end of the East-West divide and the opening of political borders coincided with the rapid acceleration of economic globalization. The financial and economic power of multinationals increased exponentially, while the power of nation-states seemed to be on the wane. The *United Nations Organization* (UN) sought to reinforce its institutions to increase its global normative power and thereby to position itself at the strategic center of global governance. Claiming that it had received an *ethical mandate* and that it enjoyed *universal moral authority*, the UN presented itself as the only institution capable of making globalization *human, ethical* and *sustainable*. It offered to become the ethical counterweight to the global economic power of the market and claimed a monopoly over ethics during the decisive years which followed the fall of the Berlin Wall.

From 1990 the UN organized an unprecedented series of large inter-governmental conferences covering all aspects of life in society (see annex C): *education* (Jomtien, 1990); *children* and their *rights* (New-York, 1990); the *environment* (Rio, 1992); *human rights* (Vienna, 1993); *population* (Cairo, 1994); *social development* (Copenhagen, 1995); *women* (Beijing, 1995); *habitat* (Istanbul, 1996) ; and *food security* (Rome, 1996). The objective of the conference process was to build a *new world vision*, a *new world order*, a *new global consensus* on the norms, values and priorities for the international community in the 21st century.

At the beginning of the 1990s, everyone was proclaiming the *end of ideologies*. According to the rationale commonly used at the time, the "end of ideologies" had put the world in a *state of consensus*: democracy, freedom, human rights, the free market, the West - modernity - seemed to have won the day and to have become the end horizon of humanity. It was, in the famous phrase of Francis Fukuyama, the *end of history*[1]. As all were in agreement about this vision, which seemed to impose itself naturally, the problems of humanity were claimed to be no more than of a pragmatic order. Poverty, environmental degradation, population growth, gender inequality and human rights abuses were seen as problems needing no real political debate, and whose resolution depended chiefly on *technicians*. It seemed to go without saying that governments should transfer part of their power and authority to *experts*.

In reality, the experts at the rudder of global governance at the beginning of the 1990s had *global normative ambitions*. According to them, the problems of humanity had become *global* and required not only global *solutions*, but also global *values*. This assertion has not been challenged, even though it concealed an evident ideological and globalist agenda.

After the cultural revolution which had deconstructed traditional western values, it was tacitly accepted that the new global ethic should be constructed as it were *ex nihilo*, that is to say as if human nature and Divine law did not exist, through a *process of consensus* (since humanity was assumed to be in a *state of consensus*) and not through the hostile confrontation of opinions which had marked modernity and the cold war.

In reality the logic of this reasoning was simplistic and erroneous. It was founded on the *myth of neutrality*, a legacy of the secularism then apparently triumphing and manifesting itself under several guises which it is worth deconstructing:

- The *myth of scientific neutrality* and *blind faith in expertise*: the experience of the years that followed the fall of the Berlin Wall soon proved that the "experts" were putting themselves at the service of hidden ideological agendas. The moral weakness of the West at the hour when it was going full tilt into globalization allowed these ideologues to grab power and to integrate their gains from the western cultural revolution into the codification of the new global ethic.

- The *absolutization of democracy* and *freedom*: as we saw in the preceding chapter, the western cultural revolution had radicalized freedom and deconstructed the traditional values which had given the West a particular responsibility in the world and a moral legitimacy to democracy. Democracy is not an end or a good in itself, and all that is western is not necessarily good and worthy of universal application.

- Finally, the *myth of consensus*: authentic and lasting consensus is impossible without *commitment* and *clarity* regarding its content. The "global consensus", which is fundamentally ambivalent (and with its ambivalence, which makes commitment impossible) is not sustainable.

The new global language and the global cultural revolution

The *new global consensus* is an ensemble of *new paradigms* expressed through a *new language*. Here are a few examples of words and expressions belonging to this language:

> *globalization with a human face, world citizenship, consensus, sustainable development, partnerships, civil society, NGOs, good governance, participatory democracy, quality of life, education for all, equal access, women's empowerment, sexual and reproductive health and rights, informed choice, gender, gender equality, equal*

> *opportunity, equal and universal access, clarification of values, capacity building, best practices, corporate social responsibility, human security, cultural diversity, the rights-based approach, peace education, parliament of children...*

Words expressing concepts that the western cultural revolution deconstructed tend to be *absent* from the global language. Here are a few examples:

> *truth, love, charity, husband, wife, spouse, parents, father, mother, son, daughter, brother, sister, person, family, communion, heart, conscience, reason, intelligence, will, complementarity, identity, virginity, chastity, modesty, decency, happiness, growth, joy, hope, faith, good, evil, sin, suffering, sacrifice, gift, gratuitousness, service, common good, morality, law, nature, dogma, response, mystery, meaning, definition, reality, (democratic) representation...*

Did not Jacques Derrida suggest, in an article which appeared in *Le Monde* shortly before his death in 2004, eliminating the word "marriage" from the French civil code in order to resolve the problem of the juridical status of homosexual couples? The exclusion of certain words is an important factor to take into account in the analysis.

The new language reflects dramatic paradigm shifts marking the transition of the West from *modernity* to *postmodernity*. The scope and depth of these changes are such that it is appropriate to talk of a *global cultural revolution*. The global cultural revolution goes beyond the frontiers of the erotic revolution: it affects the domains of politics, development, human rights, health, education, culture, inter-religious dialogue, national and multilateral politics. Here are some examples of these paradigm shifts:

Old paradigm	New paradigm
Modernity	Postmodernity
Growth	Sustainability
Top-down	Bottom-up
Norms	Choice
Government	Governance
Representative democracy	Participatory democracy
Sectoral approach	Holism
Confrontation	Dialogue
Majority vote	Consensus

Institutional power	Rights of individuals
Universal values	Global ethic
Population control	Sexual and reproductive rights
Short term	Long term
Objective needs	Individual right to choose
International	Global
Intergovernmental	Multistakeholder
National sovereignty	Global governance
Objective knowledge	Life skills
Authority	Autonomy, empowerment
Hierarchy	Equality
Centralization	Decentralization
Leadership of subordination	Leadership of integration
Power of the market	Postmodern ethic
Power over	Power with
International security	Human security
Answers, certitudes, dogma	Questions, choice, tolerance
Happiness	Quality of life
Traditional family	Family under all its forms
Patriarchy	Gender equality
International law	Cosmopolitan law
Win-lose	Win-win
National citizenship	Global citizenship
Human life	Life under all its forms (vegetal, animal...)
Religion	Spirituality
Imposition	Internalization, ownership
Education	Training
Cultural identity	Cultural diversity
Tradition	Cultural liberty
Spouse	Partner
Life	Vitality
Content	Process
Orders	Advice
Director	Facilitator
Government	Management
Parents	Reproducers
Dogma	Freedom to choose
Truth	Right to error
Homogeneous nations	Multiculturalism
...	...

The global power of some western media and especially the techno-logical revolution of the Internet in the mid-1990s allowed the in-stantaneous and planetary diffusion of the new language. The new paradigms spread like wildfire in all directions, from West to East and from North to South, from the global to the local level, passing via the regional and national levels, from the UN to other international organizations, to the *European Union*, to the *African Union*, to the *State Department* in Washington, to the *Duma* in Moscow, to govern-ments of developing countries and their ministers, to public services, to associations and NGOs, to businesses, to the media, to dispensaries and schools in Africa, to local authorities, to youth groups, to families, to local communities, even to religious communities, from New-York to the most remote African village. Not a single institution remained untouched. The cultural tsunami overwhelmed mentalities, lifestyles and behaviors everywhere in the world. In spite of its effectiveness, the cultural revolution has gone largely unnoticed. It came about *above* the national level (at the level of the UN) and *below* it (at the level of the "civil society movement").

An internal logic interlinks the new paradigms. The new paradigms are interdependent, indivisible and interactive. They reinforce each other. They belong to a *whole*, a system where all is in all. For exam-ple, according to the new system, *good governance*, which presupposes among other things *consensus-building* and *bottom-up participation* (by *NGOs*), is the way to implement *sustainable development*, which goes through *gender equality*, of which *universal access* to *reproductive health*, itself founded on the *right to choose* and *safe abortion*, is the preliminary condition. The new paradigms are *holistic*: they include each other to such an extent that they are totally mutually inclusive. They adhere to a common ethic.

Hijacking the global consensus: towards a post-democratic era?

The post-cold war global consensus-building process has been hi-jacked. The May 1968 generation were in their forties and fifties and occupied key positions at the UN at the time when the global cultural revolution began, after the fall of the Berlin Wall. Since the 1960s, while western governments were occupied containing the Soviet threat during the cold war, that generation worked within and around in-ternational bureaucracies, building networks, acquiring undisputable expertise in the socioeconomic domains addressed at the conferences.

NGOs (environmental, feminist, pacifist, human rights...), the powerful population control lobby, its multi-billion dollar industry and other groups marked by western apostasy began to organize themselves. They constituted networks which became more and more operational. After 1989, these groups and individuals presented themselves as "the" experts whom the international community needed in order to respond to the new challenges of humanity. Without coming up against opposition, a minority of ideologues sharing the same opinions, belonging to a western intelligentsia of postmodern persuasion, exercised a global normative leadership under cover of their expertise. The predominant political factor of the global cultural revolution has been the effective control acquired by this powerfully financed minority over the UN machinery, and by the UN *Secretariat* over governments.

The participation of large western NGOs in the UN conference process and in other national and international decision-making fora became increasingly important, visible and influential[2]. The phenomenon has abusively been called the "civil society movement". The concept of "civil society" has been interpreted in a grossly reductionist way, to mean chiefly the NGOs exerting their influence at the UN. In practice, the family, entrepreneurs and the Church were excluded from the understanding of "civil society". Favored by the attitude of the UN *Secretariat* in their favor, the "global civil society" rapidly acquired social acceptance in global governance.

A consequence of the weakening of authority and power of governments, itself a consequence of the western cultural revolution, the new global consensus is not intergovernmental but "multi-stakeholder". At the Rio Conference of 1992, the UN identified nine groups of "partners" supposed to "help" governments to implement globally sustainable development and its various components: women; children and young people; indigenous peoples; non-governmental organizations (NGOs); local authorities; trade unions; business and industry; the scientific and technological community; farmers.

In step with the growth of the "non-state partners" movement, what had been an *informal practice* became a *normative principle* adopted by governments at the Istanbul Conference in 1996: the *partnership principle*. When Kofi Annan became *Secretary General* of the UN in 1996, he made partnerships his warhorse. Partnerships began to proliferate like mushrooms and became culture. Today, everywhere in the world, we live in a *culture of partnerships*.

It is not governments, but non-state minorities who have played a central role from beginning to end of the revolutionary process. They were at once spearhead, pioneers, experts, lobbyists, awareness-raisers, consensus-builders, facilitators, partners, social engineers, operational agents, watchdogs, champions of the new ethic.

The political revolution

A *political revolution* has been the corollary of the cultural revolution. The agents of the revolution militated not only for the new paradigms which they wished to have adopted throughout the world, but equally for a *transfer of power* to "civil society" and "partners". They argued moreover that the conventional approach to development, going through the ordinary process of representative democracy, was marred by resounding failure. To make cooperation and development effective, it was necessary to make a radical change of approach and to fully involve "all" the social actors at all levels, not only governments.

In the logic of the *civil society movement* and the *partnership principle*, new political standards appeared: among others, *good governance, participatory democracy,* the *consensus process, public-private partnerships, multistakeholder dialogue, transnational governance networks, global governance,* and the *new multilateralism.* These standards represent at once the political methods used by the agents of social change to grab power (in an informal but real manner), and the politico-cultural regime which they have put in place, everywhere in the world.

A new form of democracy – "participatory democracy" - has been born and is already the object of studies by political science faculties. It is the product, on the one hand, of a form of rejection of traditional decision-making methods, of government authority, of hierarchies, of all "top-down imposition" and, on the other hand, it arises from the promotion of new cultural values, such as participation, freedom of choice, equality and solidarity. Participatory democracy has profoundly transformed the workings of democracy as well as its constitutive values.

The new political standards do not set out from the principle of *democratic representation*, which depended on what under modernity used to be called "universal values". They are connected *de facto* to the new, postmodern, ethic of free choice. Insofar as they do not respect certain basic universal norms, they are doomed to deconstruct democracy: the "new democracy" would then in fact mark the advent of a *post-*

democratic era. The legitimate authority of governments is in effect redistributed to interest groups which are not only without legitimacy but also often radical. Moreover, it is in the logic of the partnership principle to claim ever more political power for the "partners", to the detriment of legitimate power holders.

In a traditional representative democracy, governmental policies are supposed to reflect the will of citizens. For democracy to keep its legitimacy, the citizens' will should itself strive for truth, what is morally good and other parameters of *universality*. When these parameters cease to inspire democracy, the government loses its moral authority. It is then easy for non-state actors to grab power.

The functioning of participatory democracy is not delimited by precise rules. It is essentially pragmatic. The *raison d'être* and the objective of the new democracy are to give "those who participate" the power to implement the new postmodern ethic in the field. Those who do not participate, as well as dissenters, are excluded *de facto*.

While it was born at the "global" level (at the large UN conferences), participatory democracy is now developing at the national and local levels, transforming from within the democratic processes of a majority of governments.

Representative democracy and participatory democracy maintain ambivalent and dialectical relations. They are surreptitiously struggling for power. Their unhealthy coexistence is directly linked to the moral crisis of the West, which has rendered obsolete the concept of universality, hence of representation.

Representative democracy does not integrate or control the new political standards. Considered as its *complements*, these develop *in parallel* and autonomously. They have already acquired so much real power that they threaten to take effective control of traditional democracy and weaken it more and more. The fact is that already the activity and influence of powerful *transnational networks* of partners go largely beyond the capacity of traditional democracies to control them. "Participatory" pressure groups have acquired a status and influence which put democracy in peril. Their absence of representativity should be taken seriously and be made the object of serious debate. In a regime of participatory democracy, it is difficult to identify clearly those who govern us: participatory democracy is not transparent.

Participatory democracy, the *partnership principle* and other new standards stipulate that governmental and non-governmental actors are treated as *equal partners* within a framework establishing the common objectives of the partners and the strategy for meeting those objectives. The roles of different actors are redistributed: government becomes simply a *manager*; the private sector is supposed to take care of employment and growth; and "civil society", supposedly disinterested because it is not "on the side of profit", acquires a role of ethical leadership: it provides to the other actors - government and the "private sector" - the values which they are supposed to internalize. At the end of the process the moral authority of government is considerably reduced, all the more because, generally, it is not governments but non-state partners who are in the commanding posts of operational partnerships.

The forces ideologically unaligned with the vision of the "partners", be they governmental or non-governmental, are not integrated in the partnership in question. In practice, it turns out that the "new global consensus" has been the only objective of the partnerships: partnerships in opposition to the consensus, or proposing divergent views, did not come about.

The new paradigm of *multistakeholder partnerships* implies that all "global citizens" are supposed to commit themselves, "own" the agenda, promote it, teach it, apply it, enforce it: not only governments, but also NGOs, civil society actors, women's groups, businesses and industries, scientific and technological communities, families, young people and children, the academic world, umbrella organizations, unions, local authorities, farmers, indigenous peoples, the media, imams and pastors... The global ethic puts itself *above everything*: above national sovereignty, parents' and teachers' authority, even above the teachings of the great world religions. It bypasses all legitimate authority. It creates a *direct link* between itself and the individual citizen: a feature, as we shall see, peculiar to *dictatorship*.

The global ethic and postmodernity

Postmodern existentialism prevailed in western culture after the defeat of Marxist Leninism, at the time when, as we saw, a new global ethic was being built. The ethic governing the "new global consensus" is the expression and the fruit of the West's long march towards postmodernity: the new global ethic is *postmodern*.

Postmodernity is a complex phenomenon, still little known or understood by many leaders, which can be neither condemned altogether, nor still less approved in its entirety: both attitudes would be simplistic. Postmodernity is deeply ambivalent and recognized as such. It is interpreted in diverse and at times contradictory ways.

As its name implies, postmodernity marks the abandonment of modern values by the West, namely: the absolutization of reason, blind faith in science and its "laws", optimism and faith in "progress", individualism, human rights, naturalism, liberal democracy, national sovereignty, Marxism or capitalism, deism. Modernity, also known as the *Enlightenment* or the *age of reason*, succeeded the Middle Ages or *age of faith* (400 - 1400). One could call postmodernity, in a somewhat simplified but exact way, the *age of dream* – in other words, the *non-repressive civilization* advocated by Marcuse, the civilization which has emancipated itself from reality, which western culture has, since Freud, deemed repressive.

The postmodern phenomenon manifests itself in two forms: philosophical and cultural. Most analysts of postmodernity agree in recognizing as philosophers belonging to the postmodern movement those who, since Jean-Jacques Rousseau (1712 – 1778)[3], question the faculty of reason's capacity to grasp reality, and replace reason with the "general will". Paradoxically, the West seems to have begun its itinerary towards postmodernity from the era which ratified modernity, the Enlightenment.

The transition of the West to postmodernity accelerated dramatically after the western erotic revolution and in particular since the 1960s: the exaltation of libido, the revolt of the youth, the rejection of authority and of moral and social norms have contributed decisively to the deconstruction of reason and conscience, of democracy, of the western social order, and have accelerated the drift towards irrationality.

Contemporary western thinkers, explicitly recognizing that their object is to deconstruct reason and knowledge, sometimes even present themselves as *anti-philosophers*. This development signals the *end of philosophy*, of western rationalism and intellectualism, and puts one of the major currents of Freemasonry into crisis.

The Enlightenment replaced faith with reason, the supernatural explanation of reality with naturalism and the absolutization of science, the God of revelation with the great architect (the deist philosophy), Judeo-Christian anthropology with individualism, feudal subordination with individual autonomy, human rights and national sovereignty, Christian civilization with the process of secularization, liberal democracy and the market economy.

The absolutization of reason (*rationalism*) led progressively to the exaltation of science and the radicalization of positivism. While systematic doubt became the driving force of scientific research, modernity had blind confidence in science and technological innovation to resolve the problems of society. It was "optimistic": it believed in "progress". It exalted knowledge as a Promethean instrument of power, possession and control. On the political level, the Church and State separation of powers came to imply the separation of conscience and spiritual values, on the one hand, and of the domains of science, civil society and political institutions on the other. The calculating individual, seeking his or her own interests, became an end in itself and the measure of reality (*individualism*). Henceforth a *contractual mentality* has governed human relations in the West.

However, the modern utopia of humanity's liberation through scientific progress fell apart by itself. The promised future never realized itself. It became apparent that science was not able to explain everything and that its unchangeable "laws" collapsed apace with new advances. In its radical aspects, postmodernity reacts with pessimism to this disillusion: "certitudes", answers to questions, truth, objectivity, reality do not exist: their content is not graspable and it is impossible to know them. All is relative and subject to interpretation, so that the mind is never content.

According to the postmodern philosopher Richard Rorty, the task of postmodernity is to discover what to do "now that both the Age of Faith and the Enlightenment seem beyond recovery"[4]. In its radical and violent aspect, expressed for example by the French philosopher Michel Onfray, postmodernity goes further than modernity in its secularism: no trace of the Judeo-Christian tradition should remain in western civilization, and by extension in the rest of the world. The task of postmodernity would thus be to give a final impulse to apostasy to reach a total negation of being, reality and moral commitment.

After the *death of God* proclaimed by Nietzsche (1844 – 1900), the West, reaping the fruits of negation, is now undergoing the *death of man*. To stave off despair, postmodernity playfully celebrates chaos, arbitrary individual choice, diversity, the irrational and dreaming.

Because it destabilizes the foundations of modernity, and because modernity comes from the West, postmodernity often passes as "anti-western". This factor is susceptible of seducing indigenous cultures, which postmodernity claims to exalt. It is important to make it clear to those who let themselves be seduced by these arguments that postmodernity is in fact western – that it actually comes from anti-western westerners who, in making a revolution, have reneged on their own civilization. Further, as we shall see, in deconstructing the structure of man himself, postmodernity threatens to destroy from within all cultures, including non-western ones – African, Asian, Latin-American amongst others.

Postmodernity, however, also has a positive side. By destabilizing the "West" and modernity, at the same time it deconstructs their abuses and flaws, such as rationalism, radical individualism, liberal pessimism, authoritarianism, institutionalism, formalism. This "deconstruction of deconstruction" is of major historical importance, creating a situation in which it becomes possible for a true consensus to emerge.

The deconstruction of reality

To understand the ideological issues of the new paradigms and of the global ethic, it is not necessary to get entangled in the hyper-sophisticated reasonings of postmodern anti-philosophers. It suffices to grasp the challenges of the great themes which all recognize as part of the postmodern ideology: *deconstruction of reality* and *rejection of the given, celebration of diversity, freedom of choice, holism,* and *ambivalence.*

Deconstruction is a deliberate exercise by ideologues of *deconstructionism,* with Jacques Derrida as the principal master among them.

Derrida spoke of "binary oppositions" which characterize our mode of reasoning. According to him, *differences* – man-woman, body-soul, truth-lie, good-evil, tradition-progress, day-night, governor-governed, child-adult, poor-rich, heterosexual-homosexual, life-death – are not written in nature, reality, the origin of creation, the moral order, or simply in common sense. These "differences" would be without content, existing only by virtue of a comparative opposition and not by virtue of an *in itself.* They are unstable and changing: heterosexuality

exists only by opposition to homosexuality, truth exists only by opposition to lying, and so on.

Postmodernity *destabilizes* identity boundaries, making them fuzzy
and uncertain. All that exists is a *social construct*, hence the effect of
a perpetual process of change, moving endlessly from deconstruction
to deconstruction. The *instability* of reality is "inherent": such is the
postmodern *diktat*.

By contrast, deconstruction creates a new type of "difference" – not the
objective differences inscribed in nature, but the subjective differences
resulting from the multiplicity of individual choices: the diversity of
sexual orientations, the diversity of cultural options, the diversity of
beliefs. Hence it is no longer the identity of persons, cultures and religions which is celebrated and respected, but the freedom and the permanent possibility offered to the individual to choose, to *experiment*,
to make of one's life a *bricolage*[5] and to determine himself "freely",
even if this "freedom" is exercised *against* reality, cultures, traditions,
truth – against God. Let us note that postmodernity refers itself to a
form of *tolerance* known as *proactive*, a tolerance according to which
the individual not only respects the values of others, but is held to
internalize and *appropriate* them, without however "assimilating the
other". Proactive tolerance is the cardinal virtue of the new ethic.

The negation of the existence of a truth governing reality and morals is
the point of departure of postmodern philosophers' reflections. What
is truth? The question of Pontius Pilate is also that of the post-Chris-
tian West, for whom truth has become a "myth". It becomes impossible to speak of the truth in a meaningful way. Postmodernity attacks
"scientific laws" as much as it does reason and divine revelation. The
negation of truth culminates in the negation of reality, human nature,
origin, the given, the *in itself* ("en soi"), reason and objective knowledge. The postmodern philosopher Rorty, for example, wants to be rid
of the idea that "the world or the self has an intrinsic nature"[6].

Reason is held to be a western construction; it does not allow access to
reality as it is. Nothing is more contrary to the postmodern spirit than
"grand discourses", "dogmas" and "meta theories" explaining the world
and human history, unified views of reality, the "universal", "the" truth.

The practical consequence of deconstructionism is that henceforth it
is permitted to think, speak and act outside of any rational, moral

or theological framework, to follow one's instincts freely, to live in a *dream world*. Postmodernity makes western civilization shift from the *in itself* to the *for oneself*, from *content* to *process*.

A text to be interpreted

Postmodernity substitutes sociolinguistic constructions for reality. As we saw earlier in the chapter, it creates a *new language*, whose objective is to transform what exists into a *text to be interpreted* – a text which can indifferently be interpreted in one way or another, since for postmodern ideologues, all choices are considered neutral and equal. Postmodernity makes of language a space for free interpretation, an instrument "liberating" people from their personal commitment, from the reality of life and from "obligations" tied to the content of reality: individuals can thus *fabricate* their existence in a supposedly "free" way. The postmodern principle of *freedom of choice* is translated into semantics by the freedom to give words the meaning one chooses.

Postmodernity runs away from the "clear and distinct ideas" of Cartesian civilization and delights in semantic fog. *Not a single one* of the new paradigms which came out of the global cultural revolution is clearly defined. Clear definitions, so the experts say, limit the choice of interpretations, in effect "impose" a single interpretation of language and thus contradict the central norm of the new culture: the right to choose.

The paradigm of diversity

The process of deconstruction has culminated in the advent of a new culture, to which the social engineers have given a name: the *culture of diversity*, or the paradigm of *cultural diversity*. UNESCO believes that this paradigm participates in the foundation of a new ethic[7]. Cultural diversity is an ethical framework giving a *normative* character to the multiplicity of individuals' choices, lifestyles, behaviors, social norms – choices which one should be able to make *outside* the framework of traditions and outside the conditions of existence in which God placed man and woman. The culture of diversity is, henceforth, a state of social consensus has now spread throughout the world.

We shall see further on in this book that while the culture of diversity claims to be *inclusive* of all choices, it is in reality *exclusive* of choices made in obedience to truth. The process of inclusion presupposes, in effect, the destabilization and the deconstruction (and hence the exclusion) of identities, reality and truth. The inclusion process cuts itself from its object.

Rejection of the given and post-humanity

In affirming that all is social construction, postmodernity denies the existence of *the given*. Believers can recognize that it is impossible to reject *what is given* without having previously rejected *He who gives* and the love implied in this gift. Postmodernity expresses the refusal of man to receive, the refusal of his status as creature and child, and the will to affirm himself against the giver. Man deliberately deconstructs what is given in order to construct himself, attempting to affirm himself as absolute creator of his own existence. The effects of postmodern deconstructionism are above all anthropological. It is man, the unity of the person and his individual identity which are deconstructed. Do not some sociologists, studying *inter alia* the anthropological effects of the technological revolution, speak today of *post-humanity*?

Postmodern anti-philosophers describe the person as a *mosaic* of diverse experiences, relationships, choices, roles or functions played in the course of their existence in society. The person is de-centered and depersonalized: stripped of vocation, personality and individuality. It is in this way that the opposite of deconstruction comes about. The individual internalizes messages received from outside himself and then reconstructs himself from them, existing only as the incoherent and irrational sum of these messages.

The role of postmodern education is to construct and to reconstruct, as often as the values of society change, the social identity of an individual who at birth would be totally indeterminate. The social engineers teach that all choices are good, including the choice of one's sexual orientation. Such "diversity" does not allow the child to structure his personality: this "education" does not educate. It gives all the power to social engineers, who are free to manipulate individuals directly, without submission to intermediate bodies.

Primacy of the right to arbitrary choice

Freedom of choice, or the *right to choose* of an individual, is the keystone of the new culture. Postmodernity radicalizes freedom to the point

of seizing the *right* to exercise it *against* nature and the anthropological structure of man, *against* truth, *against* reality, *against* divine law.
Deconstruction becomes the condition of freedom: it creates a culture
authorizing "choices" previously reproved by social norms. Henceforth, the individual, to exercise his choice, must be able to free himself from all normative straitjackets – be they semantic, ontological,
ethical, social, cultural, natural, or religious. Such "liberation" goes by
way of deconstruction of the content of language, traditions, objective
knowledge, personal, genetic, national, cultural, or religious identity,
of all that is considered as "universal" and hence of the eternal law
written in the nature of man, of Judeo-Christian values and revelation:
all these realities would be "constraints" imposing limits on the freedom of choice. Exercised in the context of such an alleged liberation,
the right to choose becomes arbitrary, anti-social and destructive.

Deconstruction gives the "liberated" individual *universal* and permanent *access* to all possible choices: he can therefore develop his apparently unlimited potentialities, create and recreate his destiny, self-
determine at the whim of a moment's choice. But the permanent and
universal access to all possible choices which postmodern culture an-
nounces is *virtual* and *utopian*. It places the postmodern individual in
a dream world.

The individual ought to be able to choose, for example, to be heterosexual today and homosexual tomorrow. He should be able to choose
his "form" of family, and reconstitute his family whenever he desires.
All young people should have confidential access to the *whole* range
of contraceptives, from which they can choose which one suits them.
On the educational level, children choose their own curriculum; they
participate directly in the deconstruction of the values received from
their parents and themselves build their capacity to choose their social
and sexual identity.

Universal access of individuals to all the choices overwhelms and bur-
dens the traditional roles of social actors: everything becomes the concern of everybody. Children become their own educators and teachers. The new culture has taught them to claim their rights. In "children's parliaments" and elsewhere, they make policies. They take part
in press conferences. Educators become *facilitators* without authority,
who must learn from their students what is appropriate to teach them.
Teachers spend a great part of their time, which should be dedicated to
the transmission of knowledge, in correcting the behavior of a genera-

tion without points of reference and end up playing the role of parents. Women join the army and the police force. Men take maternity leave. NGOs make policies and influence the courts of justice. Businesses do social work and environmental protection. Governments no longer govern: they settle for *managing* the problems of societies. Often they do not even succeed in that. Minorities impose their norms on the majority. Indigenous cultures become globally normative. Immanence transcends transcendence. Everything is upside down. Deconstruction has turned the world on its head. Since transcendence has been banished, hierarchies are put in disarray. A *horizontal society* has emerged. Equality has been radicalized.

"Reconstruction"

After deconstruction comes reconstruction. Postmodern deconstruction of the "Western order" and traditions has created a vacuum in the emerging global civilization. "Reconstruction" has been a *constructivist* exercise: as we have seen, it has not set out from the givens of reality, nature, democratic tradition, the moral order, divine revelation, of *what is*. Its building blocks have been the virtual, changing and arbitrary choices of groups and individuals. Hence, the new global order is built on *shifting sands*. And yet the power of this culture has already made it *binding*.

The process of deconstruction has not destroyed, but *destabilized* the structure of old paradigms. The constructivist exercise operates the shift from the old to the new paradigms through a *holistic process of integration* of new components (corresponding to arbitrary individual choices) in traditional concepts, which do not disappear but are transformed from within. This process of integration culminates in the formation of a new paradigm held to be "totally inclusive". Hence all the paradigms of the new ethic, without exception, are presented as *holistic*.

The holistic process

Holism implies a plurality of components as well as a unifying configuration. The normative principle of freedom of choice gives a common unifying configuration to postmodern paradigms and the new ethic. When a component is integrated into a new paradigm, its identity is deconstructed and transformed by the postmodern norms. The integration process is *transforming*. It is not neutral.

Let us analyze the holistic process, by taking the example of *governance*, a postmodern paradigm:

1.- *The point of departure: the old paradigm.* The constructivist process takes as point of departure an old paradigm: to build the concept of *governance*, it starts from the concept of *government*. It presupposes the destabilization of what constituted the identity of government – its *authority*, its function of *service* (representation of citizens), the common values of nations, the social contract. In a general way, the holistic process presents all forms of identity (national, religious, cultural, political, sexual, genetic...) as confrontational, partial, exclusive, contrary to holistic logic and hence to be transformed. A "progressive" propaganda is then organized, seeking to demonstrate that the concept of government has become inadequate to the new situation of the world and that it no longer fully responds to the needs of people in the era of globalization: it must be reviewed and "completed".

2.- *Enlargement through integration.* The constructivist process then focuses on the components which it wishes to integrate into the new paradigm – in this case NGOs and other "non-state actors", whose merits are praised: the "civil society movement" (NGOs) would allow a *revitalization* of a democracy that is out of steam and the *humanization* of globalization by containing the power of the market. "Good governance" includes three components: government, "civil society" and the "private sector". As opposed to government, governance, a more "inclusive" concept, would go in the direction of social developments and "progress". It would not destroy the concept of government, but *enlarge* and *complement* it to respond to current human needs.

3.- *Redistributing power to minorities.* The process of holistic integration is a strategy of power redistribution to activist minorities (feminists, indigenous peoples, prostitutes, children and adolescents, atheistic humanists, pacifists, environmentalists...). Good governance allows them to acquire growing influence in the decision-making process at the international as well as the regional and local levels. Minorities present themselves as neglected, oppressed or excluded political categories. Power redistribution to minorities is a principle of action of "good governance".

4.- *Equilibrium or balance*. The constructivist process seeks to establish an equilibrium among the old and new components: at the end of the process, the latter should ideally have equal weight in the balance. The holistic process makes the minority equal to the majority. To reach this point, it passes through readjustments: for example, it transfers authority from government to "civil society". The apparent absence of hierarchy in the "new whole" establishes a horizontal system, an equality among components which favors the impoverishment of cultures and identities.

5.- *Transforming integration*. Holism is syncretistic. The integration of new components into the base concept is transforming. The transfer of authority to "civil society" leaves intact neither government nor business: it weakens them both. The weakening of government and business belongs to the conceptual structure of governance. Thus weakened, government and business *internalize* and *appropriate to themselves*, without resistance, the values of NGOs. Henceforth, the three components of governance (government, "civil society" and the "private sector") are unified by their adhesion to the "values" of the minority pressure groups. Holism is the strategy used to transfer the values of the minority component (NGOs) to the other components (government, business). These latter lose their identity and the specificity of their function. The revolutionary values become those of the whole.

6.- *The new holistic paradigm*. The holistic process reaches equilibrium, that is to say its completion, once the new ethic has transformed from within the values of the old paradigm. The *great whole* which is the end of the holistic process could in reality be a *great vacuum*, for the concepts have been transformed into a process of change and have been emptied of content. Yet it is claimed that the new paradigm "transcends" the old: the new paradigm is supposed to be not only higher in value than the old one, but also to integrate it and transform it from within by its own values, and to become by the same token mandatory.

Analysis reveals that the new paradigms are not as holistic as they claim to be, but reductionistic. In practice they reduce religion to spirituality, spirituality to mental well-being, human creativity to the acquisition of techniques, health to reproductive health, governance to the enlightened despotism of experts or the participation of NGOs, sustainable development to environmental protection, the human person in its rich complexity to an abstract individual whose needs, rights and values are determined by a handful of experts according to a collectivist agenda.

Examples

The paradigms of postmodernity are presented as *broader* and more inclusive than those of modernity. The agents of cultural transformation accord an added value to holism. The global ethic is held to be *superior* to traditional or universal values. Here are a few examples:

- *Sustainable development.* It integrates three parameters: economic growth (traditional development paradigm), social equity, and environmental protection. Sustainable development "transcends" economic growth after having destabilized it.

- *Cultural diversity.* It celebrates *all* cultures, "broadening" western culture by integrating other cultures into it. Cultural diversity dissolves the identity of western civilization and of the cultures it integrates, and "transcends" them all.

- *The family under all its forms.* Besides the traditional family, it includes single parent families, reconstituted families, homosexual unions. "The family under all its forms" deconstructs the traditional family but would place itself above it.

- The *universal rights culture.* It incorporates equally the rights recognized in the *Universal Declaration* of 1948 and in the different human rights treaties on the one hand, and on the other the new rights forged by the agents of the western cultural revolution – rights which are subordinated no longer to transcendent values but to the right to choose (see chapter four). The universal rights culture deconstructs and "transcends" the concept of universality.

- *Health.* It is defined as a state of complete physical, mental, social and spiritual well-being, not merely the absence of disease or infirmity. Health "transcends" the state of absence of illness.

- *Culture of peace.* It would not only be a situation marked by the absence of conflicts, but a culture where the new postmodern values are transmitted: tolerance, solidarity, rights education, participation, gender equity, reproductive health, and so on. The culture of peace "transcends" the absence of conflict.

- *Quality of life.* It is a state of *total harmony* for all, including equally individual well-being and the collective respect for the environment, an equitable society, the autonomy of women and children, access to choice, power over one's own life... Quality of life deconstructs and "transcends" the traditional concept of individual happiness.

- *Education for all.* It includes equally formal education as well as informal and non-formal education, which all address themselves to *all* people: girls as well as boys, disabled people, the HIV-positive, indigenous minorities and other minorities. Along with the transmission of objective knowledge, it also integrates life skills education. Education for all "transcends" traditional education.

- *Reproductive health.* It "broadens" the concept of family planning by integrating the rights-based approach, sexual education and the transformation of mentalities, maternal and infant health, *universal* access (to "all") to the *whole* range of birth control and "safe" abortion methods, wherever it is legal. Reproductive health "transcends" family planning.

- *Life skills education.* It teaches how to live together, to do, to be, to protect oneself from diseases, to "negotiate" sexual relations, to build peace, to change our lifestyles in favor of sustainable development and so on. The concept of life skills "transcends" education.

The ethic of ambivalence

The cultural revolution has built a *tower of Babel*. The semantic consequence of the holistic approach is *ambivalence*. Inclusive of all the possibilities of interpretation, the new paradigms can signify all and any of these, according to the ideological lens of the person interpreting them (liberalism, socialism, Christian democracy, eco, hedonism, individualism, secularism...) and according to his or her strategic priorities. Ambivalent language permits the arbitration of a regime of coexistence of multiple ideologies. Postmodernity effectively tolerates that words be interpreted not only in diverse ways, but also often in contradictory ways. The postmodern refusal to give clear, unique, exclusive content to words ends up in incoherence.

Sustainable development, for example, can signify at once environmental protection, economic development, or social equity, according to perspectives that can be more or less sensible or more or less radical. The old paradigms corresponded to unique and identifiable realities (for example, the word *spouse*), while postmodern paradigms are multiple and defy identification (for example, *partners*).

Though fuzzy, the new concepts have nonetheless become the object of a *global consensus* in the course of the 1990s. The consensus confers on the new postmodern ethic the "authority" which the agents of transformation need to implement it globally. Sooner or later, however, it will transpire that a consensus whose object is ambivalent is a false consensus and is not sustainable.

A new form of dictatorship?

The ethic of ambivalence is undermined by its internal contradictions. It is doomed to deconstruct itself. Postmodernity claims to have liberated us from all forms of authority, all dogma, all taboo and all normative straitjackets. It exalts, as no culture has ever done before, *absolute individual liberty*. But it makes of this principle a *norm*, a *global ethic*, an *exclusive system* - a *cultural dictatorship*. We are already living under a regime of *single thought* ("pensée unique"). *De facto*, the new postmodern paradigms are already globally normative. The postmodern ethic is *binding*, and this not only for governments, but also horizontally for all actors in society - associations, businesses, education and health systems, media, religions. All "citizens of the world" are supposed to *internalize, appropriate* and *implement* it; they are all held *accountable* in its implementation.

The ethic of the right to choose suppresses the seeds of potential opposition to its radical interpretation of freedom and neutralizes influences susceptible of contradicting its *relativistic dogma*. Relativism gives citizenship rights only to itself. Very often it actualizes its precepts into *law*. We can also ask ourselves whether the problem is not absolutism or totalitarianism rather than relativism. Thus:

- *A single choice*. The culture of the right to choose leaves us no other choice than that of adopting and implementing its own norms and values. *Universal access to all choices* signifies in reality the imposition on all of the "choice" of the imperative of the new ethic, the *choice of negation*, the choice of the one who has rejected the father and opted *for himself*. Radicalism is exclusive: it does not allow other choices. Universal access to all choices is therefore a *myth*. The impossibility of choosing could become the paradoxical culmination of the universal culture of free choice.

- *Mandatory tolerance*. It is *forbidden* to forbid, to contradict the new ethic. Sexual *permissiveness* becomes obligatory. It is included in the social contract. The new consensus is a new *social contract* consisting of new *obligations* and *responsibilities*.

- *Discrimination against the majority*. The principle of non-discrimination (inclusion of minorities) has been imposed to such an extent that the majority is excluded *de facto* and is no longer consulted seriously in decision making. We are governed by experts who are spokesmen for minorities.

- *Systemic deconstruction*. Postmodernity rejects all ideological systems, all the "-isms" of the past: totalitarianism; rationalism; moralism; formalism; nationalism; colonialism; imperialism; machismo; paternalism; dogmatism; dolorism; authoritarianism; institutionalism; intellectualism; naturalism; clericalism; feminism; sentimentalism; individualism; collectivism; liberalism; structuralism... But postmodernity makes of deconstruction a *holistic system*.

- *Reductionistic holism*. The ethic which claims to be holistic is radically reductionistic. It excludes the family, religion, enterprise, and national sovereignty from "civil society". It replaces them with family under all its forms, spiritualities, NGOs and global governance.

- *Rejection of power by power grab*. Postmodernity reacts against all imposition of power (male, western, majority, institutional, moral, hierarchical, religious, WASP[8], protestant, economic...). In reality it creates a new form of imposition by "oppressed minorities" - a category in whose front ranks it places women. The postmodern ethic considers all authority to be in principle arbitrary. It perceives the imposition of a single point of view as a *colonization* from which those who are subject to it must be emancipated, by force. *Power* takes the place of truth in a culture where truth is no longer authoritative. The rejection of truth makes this power arbitrary and often brutal. *Conflicts* ensue between groups (men-women, north-south, heterosexual-homosexual, nationals-immigrants...). When justice and reason are no longer the norm, there is no other solution but force to resolve conflicts. If there are no *universal* principles of right, justice becomes *pragmatic*. A contradiction arises from this anarchy since a solution cannot come about except through force, which leads to relations of domination, submission and oppression - precisely what the non-repressive postmodern civilization claims to banish.

- *Neo-colonialism of the anti-western westerners*. Finally, postmodernity reacts against what it calls "western imperialism". But it should be stressed that postmodernity is itself both imperialist and western[9]. It imposes on the rest of the world the worst that the West has to offer: the deconstruction of traditional values common to all humanity, which postmodernity considers intolerant, sectarian and elitist. Postmodernity is also a form of western neo-colonialism which threatens not only African, Asiatic and Latin-American cultures, but also the faith brought to them by the missionaries associated with the first colonization. Its devastating effects are to be seen in the domain of the family and of traditions.

Postmodernity; global ethic; global cultural revolution; paradigm shifts; the end of ideologies; consensus; experts; constructivism; deconstruction; global language; participatory democracy; anti-philosophers; the age of dream; ambivalence; text to be interpreted; differences; process of change; celebration; cultural diversity; proactive tolerance; virtual; transforming integration; holistic process; equilibrium; balance; redistribution of power; broadening; the principle of non-definition; western imperialism; neo-colonization.

[1] In his best-seller *The End of History*, published in the United States in 1992, Francis Fukuyama said that the end of ideologies opened an era in which all countries in the world were inexorably geared towards liberal democracy and the market economy, thus marking the end of history. Fukuyama had already published an article with the same title in 1989, in the magazine *The National Interest*.

[2] We have gone, for example, from 45 NGOs present at the *Children's Summit* in 1990 to 2,400 NGOs at *Habitat II* in 1996. At Beijing in 1995, 30,000 individuals represented 2,100 NGOs.

[3] Following him, philosophers who have contributed more or less closely to the postmodern process include Emmanuel Kant (1724 - 1804); Friedrich Schleiermacher (1768 - 1834); Friedrich Hegel (1770 - 1831); Arthur Schopenhauer (1788 - 1860); Soren Kierkegaard (1813 - 1855); Karl Marx (1818 - 1883); Friedrich Engels (1820 - 1895); Friedrich Nietzsche (1844 - 1900); Sigmund Freud (1856 - 1939); Martin Heidegger (1889 - 1976); Ludwig Wittgenstein (1889 - 1951); Antonio Gramsci (1891 - 1937); Herbert Marcuse (1898 - 1979); Jean-Paul Sartre (1905 - 1980); Claude Lévy-Strauss (1908 -); Jean-François Lyotard (1924 -1998); Michel Foucault (1926 - 1984); Jürgen Habermas (1929 -); Jacques Derrida (1930 - 2004); Richard Rorty (1931 -); Michel Onfray (1959 -). We give particular emphasis to the structuralism of Levy-Strauss, according to which we are made by our environment, and quote the definition which Lalande gave of structure: "an assembly, a system formed of interconnected phenomena such that each depends on the others and cannot be what it is except in and through its relation with them."

[4] Richard Rorty. *Consequences of pragmatism*. University of Minnesota Press. 1982, p. 175.

[5] "Bricolage" is a word belonging to postmodern semantics.

[6] Richard Rorty. *Contingency, Irony, and Solidarity*. Cambridge University Press. 1989, p. 8.

[7] The Universal Declaration of UNESCO on Cultural Diversity "is now one of the founding text of the new ethics promoted by UNESCO in the early twenty-first century". Koichiro Matsuura. UNESCO. 2002.

[8] An acronym for White Anglo-Saxon Protestant, an expression that originally denoted the culture, customs, and heritage of the American elite Establishment.

[9] In certain important aspects, western postmodernity comes close to oriental philosophies and religions, in particular Buddhism. This convergence must be studied seriously at a time when Asia is acquiring a preeminent place in the world and where multilateralism and the UN are de-westernizing.

THE KEY CONCEPTS OF
THE GLOBAL SEXUAL AND
FEMINIST REVOLUTION

At the UN conferences of Cairo on population (1994) and Beijing on women (1995), the leading ideas of the western sexual and feminist revolution were codified into *political concepts* and transformed themselves into *global norms* at the heart of multilateral priorities for the 21st century.

To grasp the scope, seriousness and implications of this development, it is necessary to consider it in its relation with postmodernity and the global cultural revolution: an interactive and interdependent relation links the key concepts of Cairo and Beijing not only directly between them, but also with the other norms of the new global ethic, such as partnerships, education for all, children's rights, sustainable development, quality of life, cultural diversity, the culture of peace, good governance, human security, food security and so on. In the West as much as in the rest of the world, a causal link historically exists between the *erotic* revolution and the *cultural* revolution. The new global ethic is *indivisible*.

In this chapter, we shall analyze individually the main paradigms of the global sexual and feminist revolution of Cairo and Beijing. These concepts were forged in the corridors of the *United Nations* by NGOs, experts and militant groups in the front line of the western erotic revolution. They are also, however, the result of a *political process* of intergovernmental negotiations which, by turning them into global norms, gave them a particular configuration, different from purely revolutionary ideas. It is all the more important to grasp their ideological content that they now pervade discourse at all levels of political and social responsibility, everywhere in the world.

Overview of the new concepts

Let us begin by a survey of expressions used in the language of the global sexual and feminist revolution. To avoid being manipulated by this language, the first step we have to take is to learn to *recognize* it and to understand that it is not self-evident. Following is a random and incomplete list (see annex A):

> safe abortion; unsafe abortion; safe maternity; safe sex; unprotected sex; unplanned or unwanted pregnancy; consent; stigmatization; sexual autonomy; guilt; taboo; shame; right to choose; universal and equal access; sexual health and rights; reproductive health and rights; right to sexual orientation; children's rights; women's rights; awareness-raising; sensitization; women's empowerment; non-discrimination; capacity building; peer education; the family under all its forms; informed choice; whole range of contraceptives; holism; confidentiality; consensus; sexual diversity; inclusion; emergency contraception, morning-after pill; clarification; well-being; quality of life; quality services; self esteem; lifeskills education; information; education; monitoring; basic health care; condom; unmet needs; stereotypes; partners; equal citizens; free love; right to pleasure; potential; feeling good; celebrating our differences; physical integrity; acceleration; agent of change; behavior; enabling environment; training; ownership; civil society; social transformation; win-win; prevention; for all; lifestyle; agenda; sexist violence; equality, sexual equality; gender norms; sexual balance; gender discrimination; gender disparity; gender neutral; gender perspective; gender sensitization; deadlines; realization; culturally sensitive approaches; female genital mutilation; best practices, good practices; youth-friendly services; child-friendly services; internalization; appropriation; peace education; progress indicators; voluntary surgical contraception; reproductive health commodity security; multistakeholder...

This chapter does not aim to analyze each of these terms exhaustively, but to provide sufficient elements for discernment in order to gain a global grasp of the challenges posed by the new ethic. The key concept of "sexual and reproductive rights" will be studied in chapter four, on rights, and the terms relating to social transformation techniques will be analyzed in chapter six.

The global sexual revolution: the Cairo watershed

The *Copernican revolution* taken by multilateral institutions and their partners at the Cairo conference eloquently illustrates the influence of the western erotic revolution on the global normative process in the 1990s. The expression "historic watershed" is often used to characterize this conference. At Cairo, international population politics shifted:

- From a *sectorial* approach (purely demographic) to a *holistic* approach (integrating population, development, environment, humanitarian aid and human rights).

- From *institutions* to "*people*".

- From the "*top-down*" *imposition* of state population control policies to the *individual's freedom of choice*.

- From the *demographic approach* (quantitative) to the *rights-based approach* - and particularly to *reproductive rights* (allegedly "qualitative" approach).

"Reproductive health", the key concept of the Cairo conference, is thus qualified as "holistic", "people-centered" and centered on people's "rights". The new approach is supposed to *break* with the sectorial, institutional and demographic approach of the past - an approach which the agents of change had deemed ineffective, dated and above all contrary to the postmodern principle of *free choice*.

In the past, people used to rely on the power of institutions, which were supposed to represent them, to resolve their problems and the socioeconomic problems of the world: modernity trusted institutions. Postmodernity, by contrast, stipulates that the individual should "free" himself from institutional norms to be able to self-determine in an autonomous way. It associates *institution* and *imposition*, both of which have become *counter-cultural*. Hence it is not surprising that at Cairo and Beijing, feminists rebelled just as much against those whom they called "Vatican-led fundamentalists" as against the "population establishment", that is to say the neo-Malthusian population control institutions which, in various ways, imposed sterilization, contraceptives or forced abortion on women.

Abandoning the *methods* used by population control as it used to be practiced earlier does not, however, imply abandoning the global demographic *objective* of developed countries vis-à-vis developing countries. "Population stabilization" is an imperative of the new ethic. It becomes a responsibility, at once individual and collective, to ensure the "survival" of the planet and of humanity. But the strategy shift is decisive: since the Cairo conference, all forms of coercion are forbidden, and the emphasis is on the promotion of "sexual and reproductive health" and of the "reproductive rights" of individuals. Cairo stipulated that demographic objectives would best be achieved in the framework of human "rights" and through them.

As we shall see more specifically in chapter six, postmodern methods are "bottom-up", while modern methods used to be "top-down", but the goals are often basically unchanged. The process moves from one form of imposition to another: from an *external* imposition on the person to a form of imposition transforming the individual's values *from within*, and all the more perverse that it is less visible and often almost imperceptible.

The Cairo approach took as its starting point the "unmet needs" of "couples and individuals" in matters of "sexual and reproductive health". If, following the western sexual revolution, the "needs" for contraception and abortion "in good sanitary conditions" were no longer culturally contested in the West, this assumption was not self-evident in developing countries, attached as they still were to cultural and religious traditions. In the name of "needs" and "rights", the objective of Cairo was to provoke the sexual revolution where it had not yet taken place - to make "people" (women, children, young people, the disabled, marginalized groups, *all*) *aware* of their alleged sexual and reproductive "rights". By getting the behaviors and lifestyles of the western sexual revolution adopted in developing countries, the social engineers hoped to effectively stabilize their population, without giving anybody the impression of an "imposition" from outside.

Putting themselves in the place of women in developing countries, the "experts" at the rudder of global governance (see annex B) posited at Cairo that the majority of women *aspired* to contraception but did not have *access* to it, and that such access belonged to fundamental human rights. The "duty" of the international community was therefore to help women obtain this "access".

As the "needs" and "rights" of people have been established, not by the people themselves but by the radical minorities in power, it becomes easy to demystify the idea that the Cairo consensus is "people-centered", as it claimed to be: it is not centered on real people, but on minority interests.

Since the Cairo conference, what has been at stake for international development policies has been to manage to convince people, through *sensitization, information* and *education* campaigns, that the experts know better than them what their needs are. The transformation of mentalities, cultures, traditions and even, as we shall see in chapter six, of religions is the primary goal of the agents of the global erotic revolution.

Reproductive health

"Reproductive health" is the example par excellence of postmodern *semantic manipulation.* While the expression suggests objectives to which no one could be opposed (motherhood, procreation, mother's health before, during and after pregnancy and the child's health before and after birth), it hides a radical agenda, as we shall see. Even today, very few know the real agenda of reproductive health.

The "definition"[1] of reproductive health contained in paragraph 7.2 of the Cairo document is more a *description* than a real definition: it does not allow us to clearly grasp the content of the new concept. The strategic purpose is to fog, not to clarify, the issue. One paragraph long, this *pseudo definition* includes, on the same footing, the most contradictory of choices, such as abortion and motherhood, voluntary sterilization and *in vitro* fertilization, promiscuous sexual behavior and family. Reproductive health exalts individual choice and sexual *vitality* instead of celebrating the joy of procreation and of *life*. An artificial collage of incompatible propositions, reproductive health arises from the postmodern utopia of the right to choose. Its lack of realism dooms the concept to self-destruction.

Information and *education,* on the one hand, and *services,* on the other, are the two facets of reproductive health.

> - Information and education transform *mentalities, values* and *cultures* of peoples and attack the *moral teachings of cultural and religious traditions* (theory).

- The general availability of services encourages individuals to *act* and leads to a radical transformation of their *behaviors, attitudes* and *lifestyles* (praxis).

In practice, the interpretation imposed on all is that of the experts of the *World Health Organization* (WHO, the UN agency specialized in health)[2], who forged the expression "reproductive health" with the help of IPPF experts. These "experts" thought, *inter alia*, that women wanting to terminate their pregnancy should have access to information and services for doing so. In accord with "sexual freedom" and a sexuality "liberated" from motherhood and from the moral norms preventing access to contraception and abortion in "good sanitary conditions", these ideologues claimed to have "observed" that the start of sexual activity, marriage and motherhood were social phenomena that were becoming more and more distinct and independent from each other, and that sexual activity before marriage was on the increase throughout the world. Reproductive health responds to that "observation". It codifies the separation between sexual activity, marriage and motherhood and makes itself autonomous from the family framework, motherhood, marriage and traditional morality.

To hide their revolutionary objectives and avoid the formation of an opposition, the agents of the global erotic revolution included under reproductive health uncontroversial objectives, which were acceptable to the majority, such as infant health care: as a postmodern concept, reproductive health is holistic and ambivalent. It includes all at once:

- Universal access to information and services regarding the whole range of contraceptives, the "morning after pill" or "emergency contraception", voluntary sterilization[3].
- Prenatal and postnatal care as well as birth assistance.
- Infant health care and breastfeeding.
- The treatment of sexually transmitted diseases and infections.
- So-called "safe" abortion services - that is, "safe" for the health and life of the mother, where abortion is legal.
- The prevention and treatment of infertility, including *in vitro* fertilization.
- Information, education and consultation in matters of sexuality and reproductive and sexual rights.

To justify the integration of all these diverse components into the concept of reproductive health, WHO invokes its several decades-long experience (going back to the commercialization of contraception), according to which the sectorial promotion of contraception in the developing countries where contraception is countercultural does not work. The experience of WHO, the IPPF, the agents of the sexual revolution and the agents of demographic control is that, to get contraception accepted in these cultures, it is necessary to claim concern primarily for motherhood, family and life, and to take advantage of maternal health services to transform mentalities incrementally and demonstrate the "benefits" of contraception. The aim of the integration of commonly accepted objectives and objectives which are minority, highly controversial and subversive is clearly to *deceive*.

In spite of its intrinsic ambivalence, paragraph 7.2 of Cairo has become *globally normative*. The climate of the Cairo conference was marked by a radical absence of real consensus. Sexual and reproductive health nevertheless became the object of a *global consensus*. The "consensus" was joined by 179 countries. Numerous governments, however, expressed major reservations, not least because they wanted to dissociate themselves from the radicalism inherent in the concept of reproductive health. During the implementation process, the social engineers prevented these reservations from being taken into account, so that their radical agenda dominated the interpretation of the Cairo "consensus". Equally serious was the fact that reproductive health was considered normative not only for intergovernmental organizations and national governments, but also for the "non-state actors" implicated in these questions.

Moreover, under the relentless pressure of the family planning lobby, reproductive health was placed at the top of the multilateral agenda. It occupies a central place in the development programs of the *United Nations*, the *European Union* (particularly the *Directorate General - Development*), regional organizations, development NGOs, national policies of numerous countries[4], ministries of cooperation, health, education and planning, and the *Millennium Development Goals*. The *European Consensus on Development* of June 2006, for example, which "for the first time in fifty years of development cooperation, ... defines at the Union level the common values, principles, objectives and means in favor of poverty eradication"[5], makes explicit mention of sexual and reproductive health and rights[6]. Reproductive health is now accepted by the majority of governments.

The goal of Cairo is to make, by 2015, "quality reproductive health services" accessible to all individuals of "appropriate age" (a vague concept which tends to be constantly revised downwards), through primary health care. The social engineers have repeated tirelessly to governments that they had "committed themselves" at Cairo and Beijing. They present reproductive health problems as the major cause of ill health and female mortality in the world. The Cairo conference established benchmarks to measure the "progress" of governments over a period of two decades (1995 - 2015), to the end of achieving by then "the highest level of sexual and reproductive health for all".

Cairo integrated reproductive health services into *primary health care*: this is a revolutionary gain, putting "reproductive health" on the same footing as basic health care, available at the most local level possible in rural dispensaries in developing countries. In the 1960s, family planning, maternal and infant health, maternal mortality, and sexually transmitted diseases belonged to separate sectors: the approach was fragmented. In the 1970s, family planning was integrated in maternal and infant care. Cairo integrated all these components into *primary health care*. This means in practice that the social engineers take advantage of a mother's visit to a dispensary to vaccinate her child, to indoctrinate her and to invite her to use reproductive health services.

Cairo insisted with unprecedented vigor on the sexual and reproductive health of *adolescents* (10 - 19 years)[7]. Since then, as we shall see in chapter four, the militants of the sexual revolution have launched an aggressive and perverse campaign directed towards young people, a campaign with serious consequences for the future of humanity. These agents multiply policies, programs, services and activities conceived in such a way as to attract young people. They generally define the sexual and reproductive health of young people as to do with their "physical and emotional well-being", their capacity to remain "free" from teenage or unwanted pregnancy, from "unsafe" abortion, from sexually transmitted diseases and from sexual violence.

Sexual health

The Cairo consensus integrated *sexual health* into reproductive health. While reproductive health is a *pragmatic* concept concerning access to information and services, sexual health is an *ideological* concept originating in the Freudian principle of libido (pleasure): sexual health provides an inner ideological drive to reproductive health. In terms of definition, it is even fuzzier than reproductive health.

In 2002, WHO undertook a technical reflection on sexual health and rights in order to distinguish them from reproductive health and rights. The UN health agency proposed some definitions on its Internet site, but explicitly forbade any official attribution to the agency. As a thematic field still under study, sexual health appears to be a paradigm yet more holistic than reproductive health, going "beyond" it and integrating the culture of the society in which one lives, sexual behaviors and attitudes, "healthy" sexual development as the social engineers mean it, the individual's "sexual fulfillment", the "exploration of life" by young people, "fair" and "responsible" sexual relations, the absence of disease, incapacity, violence and other practices deemed harmful to sexual health, biological risk, AIDS, unwanted pregnancies, abortion, infertility, sexual dysfunctions, mental health, chronic diseases, violence... Sexual health would also include the genetic predisposition of the individual, which seems but a step away from a new form of eugenics.

In general, sexual health celebrates vitality, pleasure, well-being and "harmony" in a pagan and Dionysian way. Postmodern culture has a holistic interpretation of pleasure, which signifies not only sexual satisfaction, but also includes the narcissistic enjoyment of "self-possession", of being "confident in one's choices" whatever they be, of "knowing one's body", of "feeling good about oneself", of "having self-esteem". Defined in such a way, pleasure becomes a system, a culture, a *non-repressive civilization*.

The social engineers seem to want to use the paradigm of sexual health to promote, from top to bottom of society and throughout the world, better "knowledge" of sexuality. Having sexualized the individual, they sexualize culture to an outrageous degree, making of sexual "knowledge" a dominant cultural theme.

The rise of individualism

The level of radicalism reached at Cairo can be explained by the devastating progress of individualism and hedonism in the West since the 1960s - a progress which was not slow to show in the policies of international organizations. In 1968 (the year of the western cultural revolution), the Tehran conference on human rights had granted *parents* the right to family planning[8]. Only six years later, in 1974, the first UN population conference, held at Bucharest, replaced the term *parents* with *couples* and *individuals* and extended the content of this right to information, education and birth control methods[9]. Henceforth "family planning" is applied more and more outside the family framework.

The transition from the word "parents" to the expression "couples and individuals" reveals the speed at which mentalities were then changing: the availability of contraception to non-married couples was already sufficiently accepted by the culture to be the object of an intergovernmental agreement, even if, in reality, it was mainly under the pressure of radical NGOs that governments accepted the change. After Bucharest, the term "individual" kindled numerous controversies, *inter alia* from Islamic countries. However, no country has ever been able to eliminate it from the intergovernmental "consensus": the radical lobbies have been stronger than governments. Since 1974, *individual* has been a key word of multilateralism.

The NGOs of the feminist and sexual revolution have militated with growing success, at both international and national levels, in favor of the *individual's* right to make "free and informed choices" – "choices" geared towards the pursuit of selfish individual *well-being*. Hedonism reached the point of pretending to change western culture itself. Woman, man, the child were increasingly becoming, for politics and development cooperation, abstract individuals, objects of arbitrary laws, cut off from their most fundamental personal relations of father - mother, son - daughter, husband - wife. Interpersonal communion, gratuitous love, self-giving, marriage, family, disinterested service, joy, the mystery of the human person were progressively disappearing from culture. For their part, in the same culture, social institutions were seeking the means to ensure *quality of life* for all - a concept which is the equivalent, on the collective level, of individual well-being.

Pleasure-seeking tended to become an absolute, placed above the life of the unborn child, above conjugal love, above family life, above love. The cultural revolution has culminated in the cultural acceptance of a new scale of values, according to which the health of the woman as an autonomous individual is the priority, above that of the woman as mother, above that of the newborn and that of the child. The new "ethic" leaves the unborn child out of consideration. Motherhood and fatherhood become incidental; they are no longer good in themselves, but means of celebrating one's *freedom of choice*. A new stereotype linking health and free choice has emerged and deconstructed the natural link that exists between health and motherhood.

People-centered development

As noted at the beginning of this chapter, "people-centeredness" is one of the principal norms of the new global consensus. "People-centered" is an ambivalent expression that can either mean "centered on individuals" or "centered on persons". While the concrete realizations of development leave no room for misunderstanding as to the *individualistic* interpretation of this norm, the possibility still exists of centering civilization on persons and love.

How have we arrived at this new paradigm of development? The increasingly marked affirmation of the individual's right to choose has become progressively incompatible with development approaches prevailing in the past. In the age of modernity, development depended on the power of institutions, the authority of governments, demographic targets, the gross national product. In 1990 the Nobel prizewinner for economics Amartya Sen redefined development as "a process of enlarging people's choices". Economic thinking, in rapid development since the 1960s, progressively moved from objective criteria (growth) to subjective criteria (freedom, individual and social choice). The world was ready, by the beginning of the 1990s, to adopt a new development paradigm: "people-centered" development, also known as "sustainable human development". At Cairo, the *interests* and *rights* of individuals became central to population and development activities, and *freedom of choice* was extended to all population programs. Western individualism then became a global development norm.

The ethic of consent

After decades of population control imposed by institutions, the Cairo revolution, it is worth repeating, consisted in the adoption of the principle that no *constraint* must be imposed on the individual[10]. The postmodern ethic of individual free choice forbids *imposition, coercion* and *constraint*.

The principle of *consent* is the foundation of the new ethic. Consent, however, must be understood in the framework of *contractual*, not loving, relationships. After being negotiated, sexual relations must be guaranteed by the *consent* of the "partners". The individual concludes an *agreement* with another individual and both consent to an act primarily geared towards seeking their individual interest or pleasure, not towards love. Consequently, is not such an act intrinsically wrong? The contractual aspect of the new ethic increases the individuals' moral responsibility. It is not a matter of simply giving in to drives, but of concluding a contract implying *awareness* of the content of one's *engagement*.

The new ethic considers whatever the individual does not control, plan or possess, such as an *unwanted* pregnancy, to be a constraint or even a form of *violence*. A child must always be *wanted*, that is to say *planned*. It is therefore noteworthy that the postmodern ethic has not done away with the modern concept of *control*, but has transferred this power, previously the prerogative of institutions, to the individual.

The ethic of consent is dynamic: it actively works at eliminating one by one the constraints of personal and social life. It authorizes, on condition that the individual is *consenting*, all that is not outside the law, including sexual relations outside marriage, teenage promiscuity, sterilization and abortion. The new ethic places individual choice *above* objective moral norms. It is eminently *arbitrary*. By letting itself be won over by the ethic of consent, western culture has become *consensual*.

The new ethic specifies the three conditions to meet for consent to be considered valid: it must be *full, free* and *informed*. The individual must possess the information about the choice he is about to make so as to examine the options. He must then commit himself "fully" and "freely" in his choice. In the new system, an act becomes ethical when it respects the subjective and arbitrary conditions of consent thus established.

The redefinition of safety

The radical individualism animating the spirit of the Cairo "consensus" has led to a redefinition of the concepts of risk and safety. According to the agents of social change, three "risks" threaten sexual and reproductive health:

> - "Unwanted pregnancies" and "forced pregnancies": the child appears as a threat to woman's individual well-being when it is "unwanted", "unplanned", or when the pregnancy is "forced"

(in the new jargon, this signifies rape committed in situations of war, for example).

- Threats to health, to "physical integrity" or to the life of the partners (sexually transmitted diseases, particularly AIDS, and abortion "in unsanitary conditions").

- Constraint in sexual relations and sexual violence, including what the new ideology calls "marital rapes" and all that it classifies under "violence against women".

Whatever their nature, sexual practices must be above all *safe*, which is to say *protected* against these three "risks". *Safety* becomes an end in itself, a dominant concern of the new culture, an imperative of the new ethic: anything is allowed as long as you do not harm the health or the life of your partner, and as long as you do not exert any psychological or physical constraint against him or her. Whatever encroaches upon this concept of safety is considered violent.

Let us note that, had the sexual revolution not taken place, the "risks" of an "unwanted" pregnancy, of contracting a sexually transmitted disease after "unprotected" sex, of dying after an abortion in unsanitary conditions, or of conjugal violence would not exist in the current proportions. These "risks" engender forms of fear created by the sexual revolution: the so-called safety culture is in reality a *culture of fear*.

The concepts of *safe sex*, *safe motherhood*, and *"safe" abortion* have been at the center of international development policies. *Safe sex* must be understood as sexual relations which are "protected" in such a way as to prevent unwanted pregnancies, sexual diseases and female mortality, as well as sexual violence. *Safe motherhood* is the application to maternity (pregnancy, childbirth, childcare and breastfeeding) of reproductive health: in practice, it contains *"safe" abortion*, but also contraception, considered as one of the means by which women reach good health, and hence a condition for *safe motherhood*.

Finally let us add that the new concept of safety has a major commercial component: "reproductive health security", a concept created by the *United Nations Fund for Population Activities* (UNFPA)[11], which defines it as a secure supply and choice of "high-quality" contraceptives, condoms and other products to satisfy the "needs" of all, in due time and throughout the world. According to UNFPA, such "security" comes through the capacity, in the medium and long term, of a given program to plan the "needs" for contraceptives and condoms, to finance the "satisfaction" of these needs, and to effectively procure their supply and distribution. UNFPA believes that the demand for contraceptives and condoms will only increase in coming years (by 23%, for example, in the developing countries between 2001 and 2015). Reproductive health commodity security is also one of the main institutional priorities of the UN fund. The UN has developed a partnership strategy with governments, donors, institutional partners within the UN, NGOs and businesses, to ensure reproductive health commodity security throughout the world, giving priority to developing countries. UNFPA is the body in charge of coordinating these partnerships. Incidentally, it is noteworthy that UNFPA now receives more money than ever from UN member countries - some 360 million dollars from 180 countries in 2006[12].

"Safe" abortion

The concept of "*safe abortion*", "*abortion in good sanitary conditions*", or "*in total safety*" (all nauseating expressions), made its entry into the global language in paragraph 8.25 of the Cairo document. This paragraph is the result of very tough negotiations. The lobby that wanted to turn abortion into a fundamental human right came up against, in particular, the Muslims and the Catholic Church, the only religion to oppose abortion unconditionally, regardless of the circumstances of conception, the mother's health and that of the unborn child.

The Cairo "consensus" on "safe abortion" states in the first place that abortion should not "in any case be promoted as a method of family planning": everyone seemed to be in agreement on this point. Then paragraph 8.25 states that abortion carried out in bad sanitary conditions is a "major public health problem" and that "the highest priority should always be given to the prevention of unwanted pregnancies". With unprecedented force, Cairo insisted on access to contraceptives and sex education. Finally, Cairo specified that "in the case that it is not prohibited by law, abortion should be practiced in good sanitary conditions".

"Safe abortion" is understood as an abortion which does not harm the woman's health and does not endanger her life, and which is carried out in "good sanitary conditions" by "competent" individuals. The promoters of this concept push for universal legalization of abortion:

they make it known that most "unsafe" abortions take place in countries where abortion is illegal. They advocate abortion services which are *sensitive, non-judgmental, affordable,* and *high quality*; *"safe, legal and rare"* was their slogan at Cairo. They do not take into account state sovereignty, the will of the people, cultural values, or the teachings of the great world religions. The position of the intergovernmental organizations on this vital issue is all the more outrageous that they are supposed to respect the will of their member states.

WHO[13], the UN agency which, let us recall, holds itself to be *globally normative* in matters of health, has issued several publications on so-called "safe" abortion to promote access to it and facilitate its practice[14]. These documents issue directives to national health systems, in the first place to those of developing countries. WHO documents and the numerous manuals from abortion lobbies explicitly express the will to promote procedures and techniques of abortion which are "simple", "reliable", "affordable", early in the pregnancy, and capable of being carried out by the woman herself or by nurses or midwives without the need for a doctor, such as the "morning after" pill or the aspiration technique. The manuals advocate multiplying centers where this kind of abortion is practiced. They emphasize that it is important to advertise these centers which, they regret to say, are still for the most part only available in urban hospitals. Their main objective is to make "safe" abortion as accessible as possible at the local community level, within the framework of primary health care. The manuals stress the importance of ensuring that the equipment for practicing such abortions is available and of helping governments to formulate national policies which promote access to "quality" abortion services.

The general principle of those promoting the right to "safe" abortion is that if the national law permits it, women have a *right* to it. What is more, they believe that women should learn to claim and exercise this right actively. They insist on women's *autonomy* and *freedom to choose*. Women are not obliged to submit their decision to their spouse or partner: such is the new global ethic's radical conception of freedom. Further, they expect health professionals to respect "women's rights" as thus understood.

To make abortion "safe", WHO recommends that countries start by evaluating their abortion services. They can thus determine where to set up services, how to improve them where they already exist, and all this with the support of all those concerned: health ministers, medical services, civil society representatives, as well as potential users of the services. The goal of the research is to reveal the "inhibitory mechanisms" which the new strategy aims to eliminate.

Since the Cairo conference, "safe" abortion is an integral part of the concepts of *reproductive health, maternal health* and *safe motherhood*. In practice it belongs to the program of the *Millennium Development Goals*.

The culture of prevention

Prevention is a dominant theme of the postmodern culture, which gives a preeminent value to the individual's *safety*, as a condition for his well-being and for the protection of his rights. The new culture is *preventive*. The prevention of the three "risks" presented above ("unwanted pregnancies", threats to health and life, and sexual violence) goes through the realization of the two goals of reproductive health: access to information and sexual education on the one hand, and access to "services" on the other. Prevention (of AIDS in particular) forms an integral part of the reproductive health "package": all is in all.

The AIDS pandemic in developing countries has served the social engineers as a pretext for accelerating and multiplying prevention campaigns. These have two facets: education programs and distribution of condoms. The first chapter showed the role of the sexual revolution and sexual education programs in the deconstruction of traditional values in the West. Today astronomical sums, which should be allocated to development, are poured into sex education programs in the name of AIDS prevention. These programs accelerate the transformation of mentalities in developing countries, where diversity of sexual orientations and freedom to choose one's sexual behavior have started becoming, as it were, "values".

As we shall see further in chapter six, the manuals produced by the agents of the global sexual revolution display a technical expertise so remarkable that they manage to give a playful, harmless, even ethically laudable and globally normative appearance to programs which are intrinsically and fundamentally perverse. Social engineering methods are seductive and dynamic. Participatory and holistic, they apparently include all social actors: health care personnel, the police, AIDS victim support groups, herbalists, traditional courts, cooperatives, secondary schools, the Church, the mosque, NGOs, primary schools, hairdressers, youth clubs, women's groups. Participants are involved from start to finish, from conceptualization to implementation. Each has the impression of being involved in a progressive and enthusing social project.

While they use apparently "soft" social engineering techniques, the prevention manuals are at the same time nauseatingly graphic and indecent. They envisage all possible cases. They apply themselves to "proving" that messages of prevention by abstinence and respect for moral laws are negative and discriminatory. They say explicitly that counselors should not allow religious convictions to prevent the person from considering "all options". Their goal is to change people's values at the same time as giving them the impression of respecting them, and to enter the privacy of people's consciences to deconstruct them "softly".

The age of dream: "universal access"

In the area of reproductive health, access has two facets: access to *information* about the possibilities of choice (the *whole range* of contraceptives, for example) and access to *services* allowing these choices to be realized. Remember that the goal of Cairo is to make reproductive and sexual health *accessible to all* by 2015.

Access to information and *services* gives people a *power* of *control* over their life ("empowerment").

Access to choices is a critical parameter in the age of dreaming where all becomes virtually possible. Postmodern civilization is *noetic*. It flees from personal and social engagement. Having permanent access to all possible choices means that one does not engage seriously in any of them: one choice is generally exclusive of the others. For example, it is not possible to engage seriously in the choice of motherhood if one wants at the same time to have access to the choice of "protecting oneself from unwanted pregnancies".

The concept of *access* connects to the great cultural change of postmodernity, which makes us pass from objective, concrete and measurable realities and needs to a subjective right to choose. The new ethic turns access into a *fundamental right*. It specifies that access to choices should be *universal, equal, free* and *confidential*.

- *Universal*: To make access to choices *universal* - that is to say to make all choices accessible to everybody - it is necessary to abolish all official as well as informal barriers to free choice: moral, cultural and religious norms, "taboos", spousal authorization, fear of parental criticism, age restrictions, marital status, teachers' misgivings, opposition from religious groups, economic and financial constraints. The culture of access sets itself no ethical limits but the principle of consent and that of not harming another individual's physical integrity. Access to condoms, to "safe" abortion, to all sexual and reproductive health services, must be universal: it is an imperative of the new ethic.

- *Equal*: Access to sexual and reproductive health must be *equal* for all *global citizens*, regardless of age, marital status, social situation, race, religion, sexual orientation and so on. The policies and programs of reproductive health are interested above all in groups which the lobbies consider *disadvantaged* or *discriminated against*: young people, poor women, the disabled, street children, marginalized groups, "outcasts", refugees, prostitutes, AIDS victims, LGBTs (Lesbian, Gay, Bisexual, Transgender)... The new ethic specifies that equality should apply not only to *access* but also to the *control* one should be able to have over one's body, one's life, one's destiny, one's choices, one's rights, material and non-material resources, political voices, employment, information and services.

- *Free*: Access should be *free*. Freedom of access implies the need for *liberation* from moral or economic constraints blocking this access. This "liberation" is carried out little by little, in pace with the transformation of mentalities in educators, pastors, imams, parents... The ethic of universal freedom of access implies, for example, that children should have the right to choose their opinion independently from the values that they receive from their parents and educators.

- *Confidential*: The principle of confidentiality applies above all to young adolescents and to women who, according to the new ethic, must be able to have access to reproductive and sexual health services and information *without the knowledge or consent* of their parents or partners. This principle cuts off the individual from his most fundamental human relations (the family) to create a new kind of "confidential" relation - impersonal, state or collectivist - between the individual and the agents of the new global ethic. As we know, the individual cannot grow without personal relations, which are realized primarily within the family.

Information, education and informed choice

The information and education spread by "family" planning associations start from the principle that individuals do not know their own needs, rights or the manner of realizing their rights. They are, so to speak, an *initiation process*. Individuals must put blind trust in, and let themselves be "enlightened" by the "experts" who initiate them to the *knowledge* of sexual and reproductive health. Hence sexual education is similar to *gnosis*.

Planning associations teach their clients that the information which they will give them will allow them to make "informed choices" in three domains:

- Choosing the number of children they want to have.
- Choosing to have "safe" sexual relations.
- Choosing to have "quality" reproductive health care.

After brainwashing their clients and conditioning their choices, "family" planning associations insist that their choices must be "voluntary" - namely, that clients must give them their full consent. The information clients have received makes their choice allegedly "responsible". Responsibility is defined not by reference to *conscience*, but to *knowledge* - a concept itself linked to that of possession and control of one's destiny. The new ethic considers that each individual has a "right to know" - also known as a "right to information" or "right to knowledge".

The information provided to the "clients" of sexual and reproductive health services is of a *technical* nature: it presents all possible choices of contraceptive, abortive, and procreative methods, their risks, advantages and disadvantages. Evidently, this "technical" information is not neutral. It consists of subtly manipulative propaganda favoring moral liberalization.

Under cover of its "technical" character, the purpose of education is clearly oriented to "demystifying" contraception and condoms, to promoting their use and to making sure that they become an integral part of each client's life, to helping individuals to overcome their fears, "shame" and "inhibitions", to "removing guilt", to destroying in each culture all forms of "stigmatization", to changing social attitudes and sexual behaviors, to putting an end to silence and "taboos" in the sexual domain, to offering psychological or emotional support to "discriminated" individuals, to gaining cultural approbation for all consensual and "safe" sexual practices, to promoting the possession by each individual of the maximum "well-being" possible, to learning the communication techniques which will produce behavior changes, to creating a "positive" environment for the exercise of a "liberated" sexuality. Oriented in this way, information and education do not respect individual freedom as they claim to. The choices are neither really free, nor truly informed.

New obligations and responsibilities

Sexual and reproductive health comprises two *obligations* which set limits on the freedom to let oneself be led by one's drives:

- The obligation not to harm the partner (sexual violence, transmission of sometimes deadly sexual diseases such as AIDS, "forced pregnancies").

- The obligation to respect the partner's freedom (the principle of *consent* in sexual relations).

The new ethic allows everything as long as these two principles are respected. Sexual and reproductive health is a *contract* which balances the *pleasure principle* and *obligations*.

The postmodern ethic - the ethic of the so-called *non-repressive* civilization - has in reality determined a number of new collective and individual *responsibilities*. "Global citizens" are supposed, for example, to become educators of their partners, to take an active part in implementing sustainable development, to claim their rights, to "reproduce" in a "sustainable" way to stabilize global population, to redress the global gender imbalance, to empower women, to deconstruct the stereotypes which hold back gender equality, to adopt non-consumerist lifestyles, to respect every individual's right to choose. "To feel good about oneself" becomes a social duty and norm. Not respecting the "responsibilities" which the new ethic confers on global citizens is contrary to the *new civics*: it is henceforth antisocial to oppose the global norms. The obligation to respect others' freedom to choose goes as far as to no longer have the right to teach them discernment between good and evil.

The global ethic insists on *voluntaristic activism*. The whole community must *mobilize itself*. Yet the engagement which the new ethic demands of individuals is a caricature. It is neither free nor personal: as we have seen, it is *formatted* by "experts". Individuals become stakeholders and actors in a global project which they have not freely chosen. The new ethic also empties the concept of responsibility of its personal and traditional content. But when responsibility is cut off from the person, from love and gratuitousness, it weighs unbearably on the individual.

The family under all its forms

Postmodernity has destabilized the concept of family defined as a community constituted by the covenant of a man and a woman in the framework of marriage and comprising children who are the offspring of their union. It has broken this "single model" of the family, which it claims limits the individual's "possibilities to choose", and promoted an "enlarged" concept - the "diversity" of family forms - a concept which would celebrate the individual's "freedom to choose". The Cairo consensus introduced the ambivalent concept of "family under all its forms"[15]. Diversity is a "holistic" concept which includes, besides the traditional family, single mothers, unmarried couples, homosexual and lesbian couples, polygamous family structures, and families reconstituted after one or more divorces. According to the new ethic, those who live together and arbitrarily define themselves as family, accepting a mutual commitment to the well-being of the other, must be equally respected as basic unit of society, as family. The refusal to clearly define the family has led to at times crazy descriptions, such as the "broad environment where decisions concerning health are taken"[16]. Whatever the form, the *small family* is presented as the norm.

It is here necessary to comment on the expression "family planning" used by countless associations not only in their documents but often in their very names. In effect, the expression, almost from its origins, is applied not primarily to parents but to "couples and individuals": a flagrant contradiction which the international community has never reacted to. The organizations promoting "family planning" have in fact never given the traditional family the place it deserves in society.

They have on the contrary contributed to divorcing sexuality from marriage, the family and life. In the West at least, they concern themselves more with sexual adventurers and unmarried couples who have formed a "consensual union" for a period of their life or for all their life, than for married couples, families or parents.

It is for strategic reasons that the word "family" is still used: to deceive the cultures of developing countries, still attached to the family as a fundamental value. Let us note however that, since Cairo, "reproductive health" has overtaken "family planning", which is now but one component of reproductive health.

Sexual diversity

"Celebrating sexual diversity" is a theme which the agents of the global sexual revolution have recently introduced in their discourse, even though it disguises old ideas which have been running their course since the 1960s. "Sexual diversity" must be understood as the normative possibility of choosing one's sexual behavior and orientation without other restrictions than the principles of consent and of not harming the health of one's partner. Since the western sexual revolution, this alleged "diversity" is understood as the attraction – "natural" and not conscious or deliberate - that an individual feels for one or the other sex, or for both at once, or for whatever sexual inclination there may be. The concept of "sexual diversity" therefore transforms into global norms the ideas of Alfred Kinsey, that we have exposed in chapter one. Let us recall that for Kinsey any sexual act, whatever it be, is natural and therefore "good". The anthropology underlying the global ethic rests on a radical sexualization of the individual.

Sexual diversity is a dynamic concept. It goes along with campaigns teaching young people that the diverse exploration of their sexuality is a "normal" behavior. The human being is held to be above all a "sexual being" endowed with "sexual rights" that society is supposed to honor and "celebrate" under penalty of being accused of discrimination. Celebrating sexual diversity is the zenith of the non-repressive civilization.

The global feminist revolution: the gender paradigm

Gender is the key concept of the 1995 "Beijing consensus". After the Beijing conference, gender was imposed globally as a new socioeconomic and political norm[17]. It is therefore vitally important to grasp its ideological stakes.

The Beijing conference, as that of Cairo, operated a major Copernican turn in international development policies, decisively reinforcing the shift under way at the multilateral level from a *sectorial* approach to an *integrated* or *holistic* one.

The sectorial approach, going back to the 1970s, consisted in elaborating development policies solely for women and to create to this end *Ministries of Women's Affairs*. However, a certain school of feminism – "gender feminism" - was quick to blame the sectorial approach for not addressing the *social structures* that would be at the root of "inequality". Half way through the 1970s this school developed the notion of "gender" with a view to *restructuring society* according to a new model of development meant to culminate in a perfect *gender equality*. *Gender* waded in and gradually imposed itself as a *transversal* or *multisectorial* issue, that is to say one that had to be integrated into all areas of development.

Gender is generally defined by the social differences between men and women which have been acquired through education, change over time and vary greatly between and within cultures. Gender feminists have established a dialectical distinction between the concept of *sex*, feminine or masculine, whose differences are written in biology and are therefore *unchangeable*, and *gender*, feminine or masculine, whose differences, according to them, are *socially constructed*, *unstable*, and *changeable*. These feminists sought to give credibility to their theories by grounding them in the "observation" of social sciences that the behaviors of men and women, as well as the roles they play in society, are determined *only* by social, economic, political, cultural and religious factors. The gender paradigm aimed in fact to deconstruct the feminine and masculine specificities written in the anthropological configuration of man and woman, their unique identity, feminine and masculine *nature*, all anthropological *givens* and in particular the role of the woman as *mother* and *spouse*[18].

The distinction between *sex* and *gender* opposes a person's body to their social function and their vocation. This distinction breaks the ontological unity of the person, who finds himself or herself as it were divorced from onseself. The woman's body and its predispositions to motherhood becomes an enemy to be fought, a reality to deny. Motherhood becomes a "stereotype" to deconstruct. The woman revolts against her own vocation. She denounces her "reproductive role" as a social injustice preventing her from becoming the equal of man in terms of social functions. She understands motherhood solely from a *social* point of view, thereby stifling its intimately *personal* character. The new ethic stipulates that women's access to sexual and reproductive health is the condition needed for their "liberation" from their biological predeterminations.

Rendered independent of the individual's sex, the notions of *femininity* and *masculinity* become processes of change and end up having no content: the new global culture is *asexual* or *unisex*, without well defined genders, "neuter", without masculinity or femininity. The woman is supposed to be able to choose freely to adopt a *behavior* and to play a *role* which, in a traditional culture, would qualify as "masculine". She should also be able to return, whenever and however often she wishes, to "feminine" behavior and roles, or to play both roles at once. At the end of the day, the individual plays out his existence without ever committing himself and acts now as a man, now as a woman, or as neither one nor the other. Consequently any affirmation of masculine or feminine identity in education and culture is considered *discriminatory*.

This "asexualization" of the individual connects to the rise of individualism; it deconstructs the configuration of the human person as *father* or *mother, spouse, son* or *daughter, brother* or *sister* – the fundamental anthropological dimensions reflecting the very structure of *love*. A woman who refuses to be a woman, mother, spouse and sister cannot be a *complement* to man: nothing could be more contrary to the gender paradigm than *complementarity* between man and woman. Certain particularly radical documents even assert that complementarity is a "totalitarian" concept. The woman who repudiates her maternal role is not able to fulfill the *social role* that she alone can accomplish as a mother. The same goes for men. Had not Freud already proclaimed the *death of the father*? And what becomes of a society without fathers and mothers? Such a society replaces love with a *contract*: the "gender contract". Everything becomes calculations and measurements. The deconstruction of man - woman unity is the most fundamental possible anthropological deconstruction. It bears repeating that after having proclaimed the *death of God* from the end of the nineteenth century[19], western civilization is now going through what amounts to the *cultural death of man and woman*.

Having "liberated" the woman from her biological determinations so that she can have access to all possible social roles, the gender paradigm paradoxically returns to *sex*. Having deconstructed masculine and feminine specificities, gender opens the door to all the possibilities of choice in sexual orientation: bisexuality, transsexuality, homosexuality, lesbianism, heterosexuality - choices which the new ethic puts on the same level in an absolute moral relativism. The new ethic does not tolerate any "discrimination" against any choice of sexual orientation, whatever it be.

The gender paradigm places man and woman before apparently infinite possibilities for choice. Without any limit being imposed on him, at every moment of his existence the individual must be able to *choose* his social role and sexual behavior. Let us stress once again that this permanent possibility to access all choices is the sign of the postmodern refusal to commit oneself. The social role becomes for the individual the symbol of his will to power, possession and control of his own destiny outside the order established by the creator. An illustration par excellence of postmodern deconstructionism, the gender paradigm expresses the will of contemporary men and women to "liberate" themselves from what is given - from the anthropological, ontological and theological determinations written in their nature - to construct themselves and affirm themselves outside this framework, which is to say often *against* it, in a radically *autonomous* manner. Like the other concepts of the postmodern ethic, *gender* is holistic and inclusive: it claims to grant *all individuals* access to *all* possible choices. Of course, this access is virtual, not real.

A Marxist vision of man-woman relations and of the equality concept underlies the gender paradigm. For gender feminists, women are still in a socially inferior position to men in all societies of the world, even the most economically advanced ones. Their goal is to redress this "social injustice". They militate in favor of a *social transformation* that they would like to be global and irreversible.

The ideological gender agenda implies a struggle against social structures and cultural and religious traditions which allegedly "oppress" women. Monotheistic religions, and the Catholic church in particular, are accused of having contributed to the construction of *patriarchal* societies and *female stereotypes* (such as the woman as *mother* and *spouse*, male *dependent*, *weak* and *powerless*, *mediator* and *victim*) that are allegedly keep the woman in an inferior position to man by preventing her from *controlling* her life and from choosing alternatives to motherhood.

In spite of its exaltation of the *individual's* right to choose, the gender ideology pursues a *collectivist* goal: to facilitate *demographic transition*, in other words the lowering of fertility and population stabilization, to the end of making development *sustainable*. Educated women who claim equal social power to men marry later, have fewer children, or do not marry: they thereby contribute to the *stabilization of global population*, as do homosexuals and lesbians.

Feminization of the masculine, androgyny and metrosexuality

The feminist revolution has brought with it an increasingly marked feminization of social norms and culture. The "feminine" has gained ground over the "masculine". The absolutization or the over-valuation of the feminine brought about by the feminist revolution has caused an imbalance and crisis of identity in the masculine, which would be retreating more and more, mutating and becoming feminine. Men themselves would now be more in touch with their "feminine side": they would wish to bring their identity and social role closer to the feminine paradigm. These tendencies are shown clearly in the so-called *metrosexual* movement.

The term "metrosexual" was invented by the British journalist Mark Simpson in 1994 to characterize men, generally urban, of whatever sexual orientation, who cultivate their physical appearance in a narcissistic way to make themselves "desirable", as a woman would do. Metrosexuality would be redefining masculinity and manifests a tendency of current culture to *androgyny* as a way of establishing a greater equality between the sexes[20].

Radicalization of equality

Most of the great cultural and religious traditions recognize the equal dignity of all human beings, particularly the ontological equality of man and woman, as proclaimed in the *Universal Declaration of Human Rights*: "All human beings are born free and equal in dignity and rights." To affirm that human beings are *born* equal is to recognize that equality is a given of creation and that universality springs from that *given.* Women *are* equal to men, even if this truth is far from always having been honored in the course of history.

Postmodernity, as we have already often said, deconstructs the given, reality, the "in-itself" ("*en soi*"), being, the origin, the creation. In postmodern culture, equality remains a supreme value, or even an imperative, but it is defined in terms of equal access to perpetually changing individual choices. No longer possessing any stable content, equality is something to be conquered - and conquered through a continual and persevering struggle against structures, stereotypes and traditions preventing individuals and particularly women from achieving their freedom to choose. This power struggle never results in the acquisition of a definitive status: *access* to the complete range of possible choices is an endless process of change.

Let us note that the radicalization of the concept of equality goes back to the French Revolution and passes through communism. Had not Jean-Jacques Rousseau already said that to be a father or a proprietor was a social privilege contrary to equality?

The postmodern approach to equality finds its most fundamental application in the struggle for *gender equality*. Gender feminists say that they do not want to make the role of woman strictly and in everything *equal* to man (which would be to fix woman's role in a single choice), but to assure women radically equal *access* to that of men to social responsibilities, resources, services, social status, power and possibilities of sexual orientation. Women must be able, like men, to develop their "individual capacities" in an unlimited way. Such a process of equality passes by way of the deconstruction of *gender disparities*, which feminists say are institutionalized in laws and social customs, and of female or male "stereotypes". Gender feminists militate against *sexist discrimination*, above all in the domains of education, health, politics and employment. Only a *global redistribution of social power* between the sexes can, according to them, eliminate the inequalities and bridge the *gender gap*.

The equality postmodern feminists refer to has a *quantitative* and a *qualitative* aspect: equitable representation of women in decision-making posts on the one hand, and on the other equitable influence of women on development priorities.

Using Marxist categories, gender feminists say that women bear a triple work burden:

- *Reproduction*, or procreation.
- *Production*, or work.
- What the UN calls *social reproduction*, namely housekeeping, the education of infants, the socialization of children, fetching water and fuel in developing countries, and so on.

From this feminists conclude that women not only work much more than men, but also carry out work whose nature keeps them in a socially inferior state to that of men. They say that a *generalized cultural adjustment* is imperative.

Feminists still complain, for example, that women's work in the home is ignored: that they have no say in decision-making, starting with the decision about the size of their own family; that they have less access to education than men; that they earn less; that there are not enough women in parliament; that poverty is above all female: a disproportionate majority of the poor are women.

Postmodern ideology defines poverty no longer as simply a lack of income and financial resources, but equally and chiefly in terms of *inequalities* regarding *access* to and *control* of material resources and non-material benefits, such as rights, a political voice, employment, information, services, natural resources and infrastructures. The "new global consensus" considers gender inequality as one of the main factors holding back economic growth in developing countries. *Gender equality* is therefore the top priority of international development policies.

The feminist conquest of equality does not culminate in a situation of complementarity between men and women, that would be respecting their specific anthropological structure. It is geared towards *gender balance*, that is, a situation of balance of masculine and feminine power and of choice of social and sexual identity in perpetual motion, guaranteed by a *contract* between the sexes.

In its applications, the postmodern concept of equality goes well beyond the boundaries of feminism. The new ethic stipulates that we are *equal global citizens*, without hierarchies between parents and children, teacher and student, CEO and employee, clergy and faithful, doctor and patient, government and NGO. A minor but nonetheless revealing current goes as far as to consider as equal all forms of life (human, animal and vegetable), which sometimes leads to the personification of animals (reflected for example in the animal *rights* movement), or the reduction of man to an animal, as we see in certain contemporary films as well as in neo-pagan spiritual movements.

Power, empowerment

The essential idea contained in the concept of *empowerment* is *power*. To "empower" means, on the one hand, to "inject power into", and on the other, to "grab power" - in other words to "promote the self-realization of". The *empowerment* of women means the action of giving power to women and allowing them to grab it - the action of making them "powerful".

Postmodern culture radicalizes the concept of power: power is not understood as *service*, but as *control over one's life*, in economic, political, family and sexual matters. Feminists see the *empowerment* of women as the mandatory path to redressing "inequalities". They consider the freedom to make reproductive choices as the keystone of women's *empowerment*, the freedom from which all the other freedoms would flow. They believe that the contraceptive pill has favored the empowerment of women by changing the *power* relations between the sexes.

Postmodern reasoning rests on a *power dialectic*. Homosexuals, environmentalists, the abortion rights lobby and other minority groups seek to take power and to become the strongest to impose their laws and their view of the world on the majority. The exaltation of individual free choice and the destruction of traditions, however, inexorably lead to chaos and anarchy, thereby creating a situation which cannot be mastered or repressed without the exercise of a strong power. This logic, if left to pursue its course, could lead to a dictatorship.

The feminist postulate is that men remain the guardians of religious, social, political and economic power everywhere, even where feminists have already engaged in battle without having yet won the war - a situation which, in their view, must obviously change to arrive at *parity, equal opportunities*, and redistribution of power between men and women. But the feminist struggle for power has been marked from the start by radicalism – by an anger or hostility of the woman not only against the "oppressive" male and the institutionalization of masculine power but also against herself and her own femininity: feminism is anti-feminine.

The different "definitions" of *empowerment* that can be found in the documents of global governance institutions do not allow us to have a clear and concrete idea of the concept. They are, like the other expressions of the new postmodern language, spaces of free interpretation without stable content. They present *empowerment* as a process of change of power relations between the sexes and of the institutions perpetuating "discriminations". They insist on the woman's "possibility to choose", on her socioeconomic and political "power", on her "access" to resources and to decision-making, on her capacity to "realize her full potential", to self-determination and to exercising her influence on the direction of social change and the world order. The more radical among them consider the family and religion as structures reinforcing the inequality between the sexes.

Empowerment sheds light on the *virtual* and *noetic* side of a culture which seeks to "liberate" itself from reality. This virtuality is expressed by the emphasis on *access* (and not on the object to which one has access), *possibility* (and not the reality), *choice* (and not what is chosen), *process* (and not content), *change* (and not stable identity), *aspirations* (and not their realization), *capacity* and *full potential* (and not commitment). The individual develops a feeling of omnipotence, a dream world where he would have permanent access to all choices, a world allowing him to never have to make a personal commitment. Motherhood and the traditional family are reduced to myths, which are moreover something of the past, while the empowerment of women, as the ideology interprets it, would be the objective they dream of conquering.

Under non-threatening "soft" guises, the feminist agenda is radical and revolutionary: it consists in organizing and influencing the direction of social change, changing power relations, transforming structures and institutions which would reinforce inequality, creating a new global social order.

The empowerment of women is carried out primarily through education, which is used to transform mentalities and behaviors in girls as well as boys. The empowerment of women requires in practice that men change their attitude and shift from *domination* to *shared responsibility*. Men must become partners of women by taking up their "responsibility" in the prevention of "unwanted" pregnancies and sexually transmitted diseases, by guaranteeing the "well-being" of their partner, by taking up more responsibilities in family life or the life of the couple, by taking paternity leave to allow the mother to work directly after giving birth, by changing the image which they hold of the roles socially expected from women. Young boys are also taught at school how to take care of domestic tasks.

The agents of social transformation teach men that they should not feel threatened by the empowerment of women: they should see it as a way of improving life in society in general. The postmodern conception of power presents women's empowerment as a *mutual gain* for women and men - a "win-win" situation. It would consist not in gaining *power over*, or a *dominating form of power*, but a *power for*, a *power with*, and a *power within* - a "horizontal" power which would be neither domineering nor constraining.

It is nevertheless worth debunking the myth of *empowerment* as a non-constraining process. Postmodern power revolves around the enforcement of the "consensus" forged essentially by "experts": stabilization of global population, sustainable development, improving the "quality of life for all", implementation of the new postmodern global ethic.

The abandonment of the *power of domination* paradigm exercised in an abusive way under modernity in relations between men and women, humanity and the environment, rich and poor is obviously a positive aspect of postmodernity. The power of domination was at the heart of *Realpolitik*, authoritarianism, the primacy of sovereignty and raw national interest. Nevertheless, postmodernity conceives the new "win-win" paradigm as a balance of individual interests, a contract without love, a selfish mutual self-realization.

Stereotypes

By *stereotypes*, gender feminists refer to images of male and female roles in society forged in the minds of small girls and boys during their socialization process, and at school in particular. Anthropologists and sociologists say that stereotypes vary from country to country, from culture to culture. They are written not only in the mentalities of the people, but also in the legal and institutional structures of a country.

Feminists believe that the dominant feminine stereotype in the majority of cultures is that of the woman as *spouse* and *mother*. According to them it is a negative, discriminatory and restrictive stereotype, turning the woman into a *victim* and impeding her *empowerment*. They claim that almost everywhere in the world patriarchal values are inculcated from infancy. To "liberate" the woman, it is necessary to deconstruct stereotypes by changing the mentalities of those who transmit them, their *vectors*: mainly parents, educators and schools, but also religious leaders, the media, art and music, games, language - in other words by transforming culture down to its foundations.

The UN, the large international NGOs, experts and anthropologists carry out studies and analyses of countries' situations to determine what, according to them, should change in each culture and locally.

In fact, feminists replace the traditional role of the woman with their own stereotype: a woman who would be a "citizen", a partner in the global ethic, fully engaged in its implementation, a protagonist of sustainable development, claiming her rights and her power, celebrating the diversity of choices, above all "liberated" from her role as a mother. While it absolutizes individual freedom, the gender paradigm is conformist, as it seeks to align global citizens with reductionistic cliches.

KEY-WORDS OF THIS CHAPTER

In addition to the concepts specifically analyzed in this chapter: Copernican turn; demographic transition; rights-based approach; sectorial approach; holistic approach; institutional approach; people-centered approach; bottom-up imposition; social change; initiation process; gnosis; global citizens; new civics; voluntaristic activism; cultural adjustment; gender balance; contractual obligations; full potential; commitment; noetic; vector; power dialectics; power of domination; power with; power within.

---

[1] Reproductive health is "a state of complete physical, mental and social well- being and not merely the absence of disease or infirmity, in all matters relating to the reproductive system and to its functions and processes. Reproductive health therefore implies that people are able to have a satisfying and safe sex life and that they have the capability to reproduce and the freedom to decide if, when and how often to do so. Implicit in this last condition are the right of men and women to be informed and to have access to safe, effective, affordable and acceptable methods of family planning of their choice, as well as other methods of their choice for regulation of fertility which are not against the law, and the right of access to appropriate health-care services that will enable women to go safely through pregnancy and childbirth and provide couples with the best chance of having a healthy infant. In line with the above definition of reproductive health, reproductive health care is defined as the constellation of methods, techniques and services that contribute to reproductive health and well-being through preventing and solving reproductive health problems. It also includes sexual health, the purpose of which is the enhancement of life and personal relations, and not merely counselling and care related to reproduction and sexually transmitted diseases." (Paragraph 7.2 of the Cairo Platform for Action).

[2] The agency produces *global health norms* and offers its member states *technical aid* to apply them. WHO seeks to position itself as the "global authority" in *health ethics*.

[3] We notice that "family" planning, part of the claim for a right for *spouses*, has then extended the claim to this right to *couples*, from there to the *individual*, then to different categories of individuals: first to *women*, then to *young people*, then to the *disabled*, to homeless *adolescents*, to AIDS sufferers, to the *poor*, to *villagers*, to *indigenous peoples*, to *migrants*, to *refugees*, to *truck drivers*, and so on.

[4] In the Tunis declaration of 16 December 2003 at the conclusion of the Fourth African Population Conference, African experts asked for investment in population programs, presenting them as *indispensable* to the reduction of poverty in Africa.

[5] The European Consensus for Development. European Commission. June 2006, p. 3.

[6] "The MDG agenda and the economic, social and environmental dimensions of poverty eradication in the context of sustainable development include many development activities from democratic governance to political, economic and social reforms, conflict prevention, social justice, promoting human rights and equitable access to public services, education, culture, health, including sexual and reproductive health and rights, as set out in the ICPD Cairo Agenda, the environment and sustainable management of natural resources, pro-poor economic growth, trade and development, migration and development, food security, children's rights, gender equality and promoting social cohesion and decent work." The European Consensus for Development. European Commission. June 2006, par.12.

[7] See in particular paragraph 7.47 of the Cairo consensus.

[8] Article 16 of the 13 May 1968 Proclamation of Tehran is set out in this way: "The protection of the family and of the child remains the concern of the international community. Parents have a basic human right to determine freely and responsibly the number and the spacing of their children."

[9] See paragraph 14f of the Bucharest conference plan of action.

[10] Principle 8 of the Cairo consensus: "Reproductive health programs should offer the widest possible range of services *without any recourse to constraint*".

[11] See UNFPA. Reproductive Health Commodity Security: Partnerships for Change. The UNFPA Strategy. April 2001.

[12] The biggest donors are the Netherlands, Sweden, Norway, the United Kingdom, Japan and Denmark.

[13] WHO estimates that there are 210 million pregnancies per year, the 22% of them end in abortion (45 million), that half of the abortions are "unsafe" for the mother (19 million), and that the great majority of women have had at least one abortion by the age of 45. 13% of maternal deaths each year, some 68,000, are due to complications linked to unsafe abortion. It goes without saying that the credibility of these figures is subject to caution. Moreover they change frequently and vary from one UN agency to another. (See WHO. *Reproductive Health: report by the Secretariat. Fifty-seventh World Health Assembly*).

[14] We refer especially to the technical manual published by WHO in 2003 entitled "Safe Abortion: Technical and Policy Guidance for Health Systems".

[15] Paragraph 5.1 of Cairo insists on the diversity of forms of family while recognizing that the family is the basic cell of society: "While various forms of the family exist in different social, cultural, legal and political systems, the family is the basic unit of society and as such is entitled to receive comprehensive protection and support".

[16] See IIS 20. US government and WHO. WHO's Task Force on Health in Development. Marguerite A. Peeters. 1996.

[17] To give an idea of the cultural importance of the concept, we point out that today more than 225 million Internet sites are dedicated to it or talk about it, in English alone.

[18] Regarding this, it speaks volumes that the Beijing conference consensus document contains the word "gender" 218 times and the word "mother" only 17 times, and these in contexts where it is associated with difficult situations such as single mothers or teenage mothers and their early pregnancies. Motherhood as the fundamental vocation of the woman is absent from the Beijing document.

[19] The expression "the death of God" appeared for the first time in the writings of Friedrich Nietzsche in 1882 ("The Gay Science") and again in 1887 ("Thus Spoke Zarathustra").

[20] See http://en.wikipedia.org/wiki/Metrosexual.

THE RIGHTS REVOLUTION

This chapter studies the history of the interaction between the cultural revolution and the rights revolution from the time of the 1948 *Universal Declaration on Human Rights*. It exposes the different aspects of the strategy used by the agents of the revolution to impose their objectives through law, insisting in particular on the progressive and surreptitious elimination of distinctions between *formal* and *informal* processes, between *international law* and *consensus*. Finally, it addresses the strategy used vis-à-vis young people so as to make them *internalize* the agenda of the rights revolution, and thereby try and violate their conscience.

The *rights revolution* was the main weapon used in the West to deconstruct human, cultural and religious traditions. In a century's time, the rights revolution transformed societies where contraception, abortion and the circulation of pornographic materials were not only illegal, but cause for imprisonment, into societies where these same practices have not only acquired legitimacy, but have become globally claimed "rights". The process of the rights revolution has culminated, in the early 1990s, in a new culture depending from a new conception of rights: the *universal rights culture*, deriving from the postmodern ethic of the right to choose.

At an initial stage of their combat, well before their claims became the object of social policies or entered national legislations, the "spearheads" of the western sexual revolution introduced a number of "new rights" into language, so as to give their radical objectives a consonance of moral and juridical legitimacy: a *right* to "free love", a *right* "over one's body", a *right* to contraception, a *right* to abortion, a *right* to "choose", a *right* to artificial fertilization, a *right* to sexual orientation and so on. In order to transform mentalities in favor of their ideological claims, these groups and individuals then fought on the fronts of education and culture. It was only at the end of their combat that they worked at integrating their objectives into policies and laws[1].

With dogged perseverance, the agents of the revolution "wove" their ideological claims into the fabric of fundamental human rights until the two became indivisible. They radicalized rights *from within*. Their combat, now subtle, now aggressive, seems endless: as their revolutionary agenda moves forward, they keep on producing "new" rights.

The rule of law and the foundations of its legitimacy

Law *educates* citizens: it teaches them what is legal and legitimate, and what is not. This education has both a formal character (laws of the country) and an informal character (culture, education and parallel processes).

Law does not need to be *constructed*. Since there is an eternal law written in the heart of all people, law must simply be *recognized* and *declared*. This law is, *de jure*, the foundation of universality and human rights. Hence human rights are *declared* to be universal.

The object of this chapter is to show that, *de facto*, human rights have been hijacked in an attempt to give "sexual freedom" a character at once legal and allegedly "legitimate". But when the rule of law does not seek truth and the common good, when it shuts itself off from transcendence, it is in danger of losing what confers its legitimacy. Democratic principles become twisted, and the consensus which binds the citizens of a society together becomes manipulative. The interpretation of laws becomes a question of arbitrary power: the strongest imposes on all an interpretation which does not take its source from transcendence.

The process of the rights revolution has been *constructivist*. The proclamation of new rights *ex nihilo* has been arbitrary. Not only does the constructivist process lack intrinsic legitimacy, but it also deconstructs the legitimate foundations of law and law itself.

Within western democracies, universal human rights open to transcendence today coexist with "new rights" which are cut off from transcendence. This coexistence is divided against itself: it is not sustainable. It has already provoked a profound malaise in civilization.

If the economy and commercial interests did not continue to ensure the smooth running of societies in the West, these might end up self-destructing.

From "universal values" to the "global right to choose"

As we have already pointed out when speaking of the concept of equality in the previous chapter, the first article of the 1948 *Universal Declaration on Human Rights* affirms that "All human beings are born... equal". The declaration also speaks of the human dignity *inherent* in all members of the human family. At the time, western culture had not yet started questioning the existence of an order *given* to the universe as well as to the anthropological configuration of man and woman. In 1948, the concept of universality had a *transcendent* dimension. Human rights were recognized as universal by virtue of the dignity inherent in all people - inherent because given to human nature by a *giver*.

However, a decisive flaw threatened the coherence of the system of the so-called "universal" values. Two coexisting visions of the world contributed to the drafting of the *Universal Declaration*: modernity, the Enlightenment, on the one hand, and the Judeo-Christian tradition on the other. For the former, the *giver* was the "great architect" of the eighteenth century: a distant and abstract god, already dead, so to speak, before Nietzsche proclaimed his death, a god who had abandoned man to himself once and for all. A deistic and naturalistic perspective was at the origin of the increasingly explicit affirmation of the individual's autonomy vis-à-vis the creator, leading to an increasingly individualistic conception of universality and human rights. Taken to its logical conclusion, the modern process led to the postmodern denial of the existence of reality and truth to arrive at the affirmation that everything is a social construct. Modernity thus contained the seeds of its self-destruction. Understood in the light of modernity, "universal values" were ephemeral.

For the others, the giver was the God of Judeo-Christian revelation: a personal God, a God of love, a trinitarian God for Christians. For these, the concept of "nature" derived from a faith perspective. The concept of *rights* does not belong to Judeo-Christian revelation as such. But human rights have become an operational concept for Christians, who attached them to their transcendent interpretation of the "natural law" and universality, namely the law which God himself has written in the hearts of all men. Historically, however, human rights are above all a pillar of modernity and seem to have been governed from the start by an individualistic logic, which turning itself into a radical process.

What ensured the cohesion of "universal values" for a period of time now over, was the shared recognition that there existed a given structure which could not be changed arbitrarily. However, the differences in vision about the identity of the giver soon began to reveal their incompatibility. The alliance on which values known as "universal" and the modern interpretation of rights had been founded was not lasting and was terminated definitively.

It cannot be denied that historically, the erotic revolution, which pushed western individualism to an extreme, precipitated the transition of western societies towards postmodernity and the dawn of the "non-repressive civilization". In effect, we repeat, "sexual liberation", which deconstructs the anthropological structure of man and woman, leads to the negation of reality, to the irrational and to the world of dream.

The arbitrary right to choose

Postmodernity, which exalts individual freedom, connects rights to *individual choices*. These become an absolute principle and the new point of reference of law and human rights, making their content unstable, fuzzy and ambivalent. We formerly believed that rights had stable, clear, precise, definite and consensual content, because they sprang from an unchangeable truth about human nature. The cultural revolution turned rights into a dynamic, subjective and confrontational process of change, allowing intrinsically contradictory choices. Hence for example some apply the *right to life* to the unborn child threatened to be aborted, and others to the woman wishing to abort. The content of human rights can no longer be taken for granted. In step with the secularization of western culture, human rights have become less and less consensual, more and more confrontational.

The *right to choose* opened a Pandora's box: new rights flowing from the arbitrary exercise of freedom have proliferated in all directions. All that becomes socially permitted becomes the object of law. The present cultural tendency is to claim as many rights as there are possible choices: the right to die or to choose one's death, the right not to be born[2], the right to a wanted child (assisted procreation), the right to suppress the child which is not wanted (the right to abortion), the right to sexual orientation (rights of lesbians and homosexuals), the right to modify religious texts deemed to be discriminatory, the right to feel good about oneself, the right to adoption for homosexual couples, the right to pleasure, the "right to know", the right to error, the right to "confidentiality" for adolescents, children's right to their own "opinion", the right to sex outside marriage, the right to "freedom to safe love" in all its forms. The culture of the right to choose has spread to all social categories, to all generations, concerning itself particularly with groups who are deemed to be the object of discrimination: women, young people, children, disabled people, indigenous peoples, AIDS patients and so on.

The right to choose is not only a *value* of postmodernity: it claims for itself a *global normative authority*. As a *norm*, the right to choose is placed *above* all transcendent principles: it incorporates transcendence and turns it into an immanent process.

Following the western cultural revolution, human rights have become the sole standing frame of reference for ethical and universal norms. But what would become of ethics if human rights were themselves cut off from a stable frame of reference and became dependent only on arbitrary collective judgment?

The itinerary of the rights revolution at the multilateral level

Let us review briefly the stages of the journey which has led multilateral organizations to include the agenda of the erotic revolution in their rights approach.

Let us recall that two years after the adoption, in 1966, of the two main human rights treaties (*Covenant on Civil and Political Rights* and *Covenant on Economic, Social and Cultural Rights*), the first UN conference on human rights, held at Tehran in 1968, granted *parents*, in article 16, "a basic human right to determine freely and responsibly the number and the spacing of their children". At Bucharest in 1974, the first UN conference on population granted the right to birth control no longer to parents, but to *couples* and *individuals*. The "right to *family* planning" was henceforth applied increasingly outside the framework of the family. From then on the international community would never again use the term "parents" in relation to this "right". The expression "right of couples and individuals", which links human rights and the objectives of the sexual revolution, is the one which successive UN conferences, including that of Cairo, would use.

From the 1970s there were no promoters and defenders of human rights more aggressive than the feminist lobby and the birth control and abortion industry lobbies. Under their pressure, women's rights and the hidden agenda they contained became one of the institutional priorities of international organizations.

In 1982 the IPPF, active behind the scenes of UN conferences since 1968, held its first working session on the *right to family planning*. Since then, the organization and its institutional partners at the UN and elsewhere have been increasingly gearing towards the adoption of a holistic development strategy centered principally on rights - a strategy which would culminate, in the 1990s, in the *universal rights culture* of the 1993 Vienna human rights conference and the *rights-based approach* of the Vienna and Cairo conferences.

The *rights-based approach* strategy has two components. The first is the integration into human rights of the objectives of the erotic revolution - an integration which has definitively destabilized the content of universal human rights. The second is the integration of socioeconomic development into human rights, so that each issue (food security, housing, education, health...) be henceforth approached from the standpoint of rights and individual freedom to choose, as understood by the postmodern ethic, and no longer in their concrete and objective reality. The *rights-based approach* has become the conceptual framework of the human development process and clarifies the meaning to be given to the expression "people-centered development", namely "development centered on *individuals as rights holders*", on individuals who are "free to choose". The UN explains that according to the new conceptual framework, a right which is not respected comes down to a violation which must be corrected by law. In other words, the rights-based approach is a way of making the postmodern ethic globally normative.

The expressions "Copernican turn" or "watershed" have been used to characterize the new approach - the rights approach. The importance of this watershed cannot be overstressed to understand postmodernity. The transformation that took place after the end of the cold war, making western culture shift from *institutions* to *people*, represents a decisive and irreversible change which has, as we have understood, been hijacked. Never, since the end of the cold war, has there been so much talk about human rights. The new global culture is a *rights culture*. But what is the content of this culture? Have not human dignity, human rights, the freedom to choose, equality, non-discrimination, tolerance, often become, in this new culture, enemies of the good of the person, the human community, traditional and religious cultures and divine revelation? Does not the rights-based culture go as far as to oppose and wish to replace *charity*, which would allegedly be "unreliable" because it is not juridically binding? Does not the so-called "people-centered" culture reject charity?

The Vienna conference declared that rights were a *universal norm* (note it does not speak of *universal "values"*), independently from the standards established by sovereign states: human rights would be *above* national sovereignty. Preparing the ground for the interpretation that the Cairo conference would make a year later of women's rights, Vienna particularly insisted that women's rights constituted "an inalienable, integral and indivisible part of universal human rights", requiring special attention.

The rights revolution led, at Cairo, to a global consensus on *reproductive rights*, the culminating expression of the postmodern *right to choose*. Abandoning the demographic approach, the prime objective of Cairo was to teach people to claim their "rights" proactively. Cairo equally established the *interdependence* of socioeconomic development and human rights: the Cairo "consensus" stipulates that development goes through the implementation of reproductive rights.

Cairo: reproductive rights

The Cairo document does not define reproductive rights (paragraph 7.3) any more clearly than it "defines" reproductive health (paragraph 7.2):

> "Reproductive rights embrace *certain* human rights[3] that are already recognized in national laws, international human rights documents and *other relevant United Nations consensus documents*. These rights rest on the recognition of the basic right of all *couples and individuals* to decide freely and responsibly the number, spacing and timing of their children and to have the information and means to do so, and the right to attain the highest standard of sexual and reproductive health."

While excusing ourselves for being repetitious, due to the fact that this chapter applies to rights some themes which have already been addressed in preceding chapters, we note that the description of reproductive rights is, intentionally, vague and ambivalent: it obeys the postmodern principle of the free interpretation of language according to the individual's arbitrary choices. It does not specify which are the rights already recognized in national legislations, international documents and consensus documents which it refers to, which consensus documents are meant, and if the "right to attain the highest level of sexual health" is equivalent to what homosexual pressure groups understand by *sexual rights* - namely, *inter alia*, the right to sexual orientation. The agents of social transformation speak of a "constellation of rights", and attribute to themselves the function of "clarifying" these rights while following their own ideological choices.

In a general manner, *reproductive rights* means *rights to reproductive health*, hence rights to all that is covered by reproductive health, what is authentically consensual as well as what is radical: rights to motherhood as well as to abortion (where it is legal), to *in vitro* fertilization as well as voluntary sterilization, to the exercise of sexuality within the framework of traditional marriage as well as in promiscuity. Reproductive rights imply a combat against female genital mutilation, early marriage, forced marriage, polygamy, institutionalized discrimination, incest, violence against women, sexual abuses, forced prostitution, lack of access to education for girls and young mothers, and trafficking of women as well as for the globalization of "sexual liberation". But since reproductive rights belong to "couples and individuals", not to parents, it goes without saying that they are conceived principally to be claimed outside the framework of marriage. The new ethic prevails: all is permitted within the framework of mutual consent and safety - except that of the unborn child.

Like reproductive health, reproductive rights have two components: rights to access to *information* and to *education* on the one hand, and rights to *services* on the other. The Cairo program of action (7.3) specifies that the promotion of the responsible exercise of reproductive rights should be the basic foundation of governments' and communities' reproductive health policies and programs: a practical consequence of the "rights approach".

Sexual rights

Cairo did not speak explicitly of *sexual rights*[4] as such, but its pseudo-definition of reproductive rights included the *right to sexual health*. The expression "sexual and reproductive rights" has nevertheless become indivisible in the language of NGOs and international organizations following Cairo. Sexual rights means rights to sexual health. The concept is as vague as is sexual health. In a general way, it is possible to affirm that reproductive rights are more operational and technical concepts (access to information and services) than sexual rights, which are more ideological: hedonism, right to pleasure, whatever one's age, health situation, legal status or sexual orientation (married, single, heterosexual, homosexual, lesbian, bisexual, transsexual, handicapped, prostitute etc.).

In the final analysis, sexual and reproductive rights are indissociable and both contain the program of the sexual revolution, in their practical as well as their ideological aspects: the right to sexual orientation, to a permissive "sexual education", to "physical integrity", to "control" one's sexual life, to voluntary sterilization, to "confidentiality" of information and services for young people and adolescents (a confidentiality which means in the language of Cairo "without the knowledge or consent of parents"), the right to determine one's own sexual behavior, to protect oneself against sexually transmitted diseases and "unwanted pregnancies", to promote one's sexual and reproductive health, to choose one's partners, to respect one's "physical integrity", to plan one's family, to have extramarital relations, to be free from all discrimination, coercion or violence in one's sexual life and sexual decisions, to abort "safely" where abortion is legal, to expect and demand "equality", full consent, mutual respect and shared responsibility in sexual relations (to have "consensual" sex), to take decisions in matters of procreation (number, timing and spacing of children), to have free access to information, contraception and other means of exercising one's choices, to have pleasure in sexual relations, to have access to reproductive health care in spite of financial difficulties... The defenders of sexual and reproductive rights agree in recognizing that their content is constantly susceptible to change, in function of new possibilities which could present themselves. Some of them publicly claim a right to "safe" abortion, accessible and legal throughout the world, a right which would be recognized as a women's right and therefore as a fundamental human right.

Highly controversial, sexual and reproductive rights have not formally entered into international treaties. In practice, however, the interpretation of fundamental and universal human rights is dominated by the highly powerful global sexual revolution lobby. Its agents are tireless and use circuitous and subterranean paths. They argue that sexual and reproductive rights have been included in the universal human rights since their inception and that they are only "clarifying" them. Their "self-evident" logic is that human rights include the rights of women, children, the disabled, and indigenous peoples, which include sexual and reproductive rights, which in turn include the right to "safe" abortion and all the "rights" we have listed in the last paragraph. Not only is this logic that of the militants, such as the *Center for Reproductive Rights*, but the large international human rights NGOs, such as *Amnesty International* or *Human Rights Watch*, form an interpretation of women's rights which is at the least ambivalent, as if the integration of radical rights in the universal rights was "natural" and did not need to be submitted to an open democratic debate. Some of these NGOs openly promote the sexual rights of lesbians, homosexuals, bisexuals and transsexuals. They treat the application of sexual and reproductive rights for all as an objective in itself, which does not require justification.

A year after Cairo, the Beijing conference, in its paragraph 96, implicitly integrated sexual and reproductive rights in what the radical lobbies want to be understood by "women's rights": "The human rights of women include their right to have control over and decide freely and responsibly on matters related to their sexuality, including sexual and reproductive health, free of coercion, discrimination and violence." Since Cairo and Beijing, the "international community" has accepted, in some cases tacitly, in others openly, that sexual and reproductive rights form part of the rights of women and hence of human rights, and that sexual and reproductive rights are essential for women to exercise all their other rights.

The rights revolution has consolidated the gains of the cultural revolution by granting them a juridical basis (when the new rights penetrate formally into national or international law) or a pseudo-juridical basis. The cultural revolution has integrated artificially constructed and often anti-natural rights into the body of rights rooted in the nature of man and woman. It has thereby destabilized the content of human rights, whose interpretation can no longer be taken for granted.

In addition, let us note that the new rights have become *norms of development*. Propaganda teaches that their application contains great advantages for the economic and social life of a community and for the future of the planet. Citizens' access to "reproductive choices" is held to be the key to the progress of nations, the very foundation of sustainable development. It would appear that respecting sexual and reproductive rights is the most effective contribution to eliminating poverty. National development laws and policies should, then, implicitly or explicitly, take them into account and give them priority. Through its *Department of Reproductive Health and Research*, WHO examines national and international laws and policies in the area of reproductive health to "help" governments align themselves with UN norms.

The pioneering role of the IPPF: The Charter of Sexual and Reproductive Rights

In this chapter on rights, it is useful to return to the IPPF. IPPF was a pioneer in the cultural movement which transformed "free love", access to contraception, access to abortion and *in vitro* fertilization into *rights*.

In 1995, one year after the Cairo conference, the *General Assembly* of the IPPF adopted a *Charter of Sexual and Reproductive* Rights - a key strategic document of the global rights revolution. Spread throughout the world, translated into numerous languages, the Charter uses to its benefit and reinterprets twelve rights drawn from the 1948 *Universal Declaration on Human Rights* and other instruments of international law[5]. The objective of the "Charter" is to "demonstrate" that the human rights treaties, conventions and declarations of the UN intrinsically contain the programs of sexual and reproductive rights as the IPPF interprets them. The goal is also to provide activists with tools with which to denounce alleged "violations" of sexual and reproductive rights in the world and to "monitor" governments in their implementation of the Cairo and Beijing goals.

The Charter attributes the *right to life*, for example, to people who are born and passes over in silence the right to life of unborn children, called "fetuses"[6]. For the IPPF, the right to life includes the right to "safe" abortion, in the measure in which the woman's right to life can be "violated" when she does not have access to "safe" abortion services. Reflecting the incoherence of the new ethic, the Charter nevertheless combats fertility control policies when they are imposed on certain races to the end of eliminating them. It also combats the killing of girl children founded on a cultural preference for boys.

The *right to liberty and security of the person* includes for the IPPF the freedom to "control" and to "enjoy" one's sexual and reproductive life in the measure that, in doing so, one does not violate the partner's rights (sexual abuse, violence). Let us recall that the "informed consent" of the individual and his safety are the absolute values of the new ethic: one can do whatever one likes, including sterilizing others or oneself, as long as one does not exercise constraints on oneself or one's partner and that one does not put one's life or health, or those of one's partner, in danger. The Charter explains that the right to freedom can be used to campaign equally against unwanted abortion as against unwanted pregnancy: the woman's individual choice takes precedence over life. The IPPF also encourages the use of this right to campaign against all beliefs (both cultural and religious) which, according to the IPPF, could engender fear, guilt and shame and which would thus diminish the freedom and the capacity of an individual to "enjoy" their sexual relations.

The IPPF interprets the *right to equality and to be free from all forms of discrimination* in such a way as to militate in favor of laws forbidding discrimination against minorities, notably homosexuals. For the IPPF, it is against this right for a woman to have to seek her husband's authorization in order to gain access to sexual and reproductive health services (and to all that the IPPF includes in these services) or for young people to be required to ask the consent of their parents to gain such access.

The *right to privacy* includes for the IPPF the right of every individual to make "autonomous" decisions about their sexual life, including the decision for women to have recourse to "safe" abortion, as well as the right to have access to confidential information. According to the IPPF, the *right to privacy* could be used to campaign against any "persecution" that might be inflicted on individuals by reason of their sexual orientation or through laws or practices requiring the consent of the spouse or parents for women or young people to have access to contraception and abortion.

The IPPF uses the *right to freedom of thought* to encourage an interpretation of religious, philosophical and cultural texts which is favorable to "freedom of thought and expression" in the domain of health and sexual and reproductive rights. The IPPF wishes to open the possibility of this right being invoked to combat restrictions to information and reproductive health services founded on moral or religious grounds. We note that it seems to be in the logic of the interpretation the IPPF makes of this right that all directive moral teaching, all spiritual direction tending to restrict sexual freedom become contrary to the right to freedom of thought. The IPPF limits the right to conscientous objection to cases where the doctor or nurse, in refusing to procure contraception or abortion, is able to direct the patient to a service where she may obtain them.

The IPPF believes that young people in particular should be able to claim the *right to information and education* to assure themselves of access to "complete" sexual information and education, that is to say covering the whole range of contraceptives, medically assisted procreation, sterilization and abortion. Information, insists the IPPF, should be free from all "stereotypes".

The *right to choose whether or not to marry and to found and plan a family* is interpreted in such a way as to make possible all forms of family planning - contraceptives as well as infertility treatments of whatever type. It is also interpreted in such a way as to resolve the problem of what the IPPF calls "forced pregnancies" by assuring rape victims the right to abortion.

Through the *right to decide whether or when to have children*, the IPPF wishes that information, reproductive health education and services, "safe" motherhood, and "safe" abortion become *accessible, affordable* and *practical*. The IPPF specifies that these services should offer the greatest possible range of fertility control methods which are "safe" and effective. The adoption of children by homosexuals and lesbians is inscribed in the logic of this right.

The *right to the benefits of scientific progress* becomes the right to access the benefits of all contraceptive and abortive technologies and to infertility treatment based on scientistic ethics.

The *right to freedom of assembly and political participation* is used to campaign against the alleged "persecution" by organizations which seek to influence politics in a direction contrary to the IPPF, tacitly understood as the pro-life and pro-family lobbies and institutions such as the Catholic Church.

Finally, the IPPF reinterprets to its own advantage the *right to be free from torture and ill treatment* and the *right to health and health-protection services*, by specifying that the services should be "comprehensive", financially and geographically accessible, confidential and respectful of the "dignity"[7] and comfort of the user.

The IPPF Federation encourages militant NGOs to pressure governments to implement sexual and reproductive rights. It proposes to them a model plan of action. The first stage consists in carrying out a "diagnosis" of legislation, policies and practices of a given country: are they permissive or on the contrary restrictive and hostile to the Cairo objectives? At a second stage, the IPPF invites the NGOs to identify their own priorities for action in that country (access to "safe" abortion? Adolescents' access to contraception?). The IPPF encourages them to document "violations"[8] of sexual and reproductive rights in the given country, by gathering statistics and concrete examples. Then comes the time to pressure governments to "honor" the alleged commitments they made at Cairo and Beijing. This pressure is exerted through the media, NGO networks, informal and invisible partnerships, with officials and parliamentarians who are favorable to sexual and reproductive rights.

The Charter offers the IPPF not only a *pseudo-juridical* framework (whence the use of the word "Charter" for a document which is nothing but a propaganda and action tool) for the accomplishment of what the federation considers to be its mandate, but it also claims to offer an *ethical framework* for the global realization of the Cairo conference and sexual and reproductive health. The Charter aims above all to give moral legitimacy to sexual and reproductive rights. It thereby radically redefines ethics.

An NGO such as the IPPF has no juridical legitimacy with which to impose its interpretation of rights on states. It would however be naive and irresponsible to under-estimate the long-term influence of the constant pressure from sexual and reproductive rights lobbies on states and international law.

From "consensus" to international law?

Since the Cairo and Beijing "consensus", the efforts of sexual and reproductive rights activists have been directed towards their *universal implementation*. Ingeniously and with unfailing perseverance, they have sought the means to *constrain* states to enforce "rights" which have not formally entered international law. They have tried to transform a *consensus*, which is not binding on states, into *international law*, which is. They have also presented an inexisting consensus (the *radical agenda of a minority*) as a *global consensus*, that is to say as the will of the majority.

To exist formally and to bind a state juridically, a right must be the object of a law promulgated nationally following an open democratic process on the content of the law, or have entered international law after a regular procedure which clearly determines its content. The militants of the erotic revolution have circumvented this democratic process and proceeded in such a way as to impede open debate on the radical agenda which they wished to impose as a *diktat*. The rights revolution has been a historic exercise of manipulation of the majority by minorities. It has led to a regime of governance of democracies by NGOs, "experts", pressure groups and other processes parallel to traditional demographic processes.

The formal and explicit entry of sexual and reproductive rights into international law is a strategic objective which cannot be achieved immediately. The militants of the rights revolution are aware that the realization of that goal necessarily goes through a progressive transformation of mentalities. Their tactics have come in many forms. They have exploited every opportunity opening up in their favor, be it in culture or in formal juridical mechanisms.

The advantage of hijacking human rights was evident. Human rights are recognized as *universal* (applicable to all human beings without exception), *inalienable* (one may never take them away from anybody), *indivisible* (all rights have an equal status; they cannot be hierarchized; denying one right amounts to denying all rights), *interdependent* (equal in importance: one cannot enjoy one without enjoying all). Human rights are the foundation of the rule of law. Making sexual and reproductive rights pass for fundamental rights amounts to making them pass for universal and inalienable rights, to making them interdependent and indivisible from rights with a binding character, if not juridically at least morally, and to re-founding the rule of law on the individual freedom of choice. By "weaving" sexual and reproductive rights into universal human rights, the activists of the revolution have used the "uncontested" moral authority of universal rights to force the application of their particular interests.

To achieve their goals, the social engineers have sought to surreptitiously erase the distinction between *consensus* and *international law*. The have acted as if the consensus was effectively binding. They have insisted without letup on the "obligation" of governments to honor the "commitments" they had made at Cairo and Beijing. Shamelessly, they have spoken of sexual and reproductive rights as if they were fundamental rights, universally recognized and which, as such, already had binding force over states[9]. They deliberately ignored or passed over in silence the purely *consensual* nature of these rights, as well as the absence of real consensus on their content (let us remember that numerous governments have expressed serious reservations).

The agents of social transformation present sexual and reproductive rights as a "constellation of rights" which merely spell out or "clarify" the content of socioeconomic rights[10], already recognized in the *Universal Declaration* (1948) as in the *Covenant on Economic, Social and Cultural Rights* (1966), the *Convention on the Elimination of All Forms of Discrimination against Women*[11] (1979), the *Convention on the Rights of Children* (1989) and other human rights treaties[12]. In other words, sexual and reproductive rights must be seen not as new rights, but as a constitutive element, present from the start within the universal human rights recognized by the international community, such as the right to life and to survival, the right to personal freedom and security, the right to education, the right to equal treatment, the right to equality and to freedom from all forms of discrimination, the right to freedom of thought and so on. On the European level, the *European Charter of Fundamental Rights* (2000) would contain sexual and reproductive rights implicitly, according to the activists, and especially in its mention of the right to life, freedom and security, information, health, education, privacy and family.

The agents of the revolution have developed a variety of intermediary tactics with which to integrate their objectives into formal juridical processes. Let us give some examples. They strive to incorporate reproductive rights into the laws and constitutions of a critical mass of states, hoping thereby to eventually bring about a shift in international law. They push regional organizations to integrate these rights into regional treaties, as they have done for example for the *Protocol on the Rights of Women* of the *African Union*. They exert continual pressure on the treaties' *monitoring bodies*. They use moral blackmail, consisting in presenting the Cairo consensus as the *global conscience* in matters of human rights. They promote a *rights culture*, an approach to development centered on rights and *rights education* which place reproductive rights at the heart of fundamental rights. To win non-western cultures to their cause, they seek to demonstrate to them that reproductive rights are not the privilege of western culture, but that each culture recognizes them as important. They "educate" the signatory states of international human rights treaties, treaty monitoring bodies, NGOs, civil society to see a "natural link" between sexual and reproductive rights and the treaties' provisions. They want to convince people that in recent decades the majority of nations have recognized and accepted the right to reproductive health, and that there exist several international legal instruments which demand the protection of this "right".

To surreptitiously align the interpretation of international law with the radical objectives hidden in the consensus of the major UN conferences of the 1990s, the UN and the agents of the global erotic revolution insist on the *synergies* allegedly existing among the international legal instruments, such as the *Convention on the Elimination of All Forms of Discrimination against Women* and the platforms for action of the conferences. According to them, there are, in principle, no substantial differences in content between international law and the consensus of the conferences. Law and the various consensus would be *complementary* and interdependent in the implementation of a single and identical task, with the UN conferences elaborating a program of action allowing a concrete and direct application of the law. The manipulative character of this affirmation often goes unnoticed. There exist in effect not only major differences of content between these two types of document, but also the law has a "formal" legitimacy which a consensus does not have. Similarly, the defenders of sexual and reproductive rights deliberately make no distinction between the *United Nations Charter*, the *Universal Declaration*, the human rights treaties, and the growing influence exerted on the interpretation of rights by the global women's rights movement, to create the belief that they all share the same vision.

Treaty monitoring bodies

Let us recall that international treaties are provided with a monitoring organ or "Treaty Monitoring Body", a committee made up of experts, whose mandate is to monitor states' application of treaties. Treaties impose legal obligations on signatory states - obligations for which they must account to the UN in their periodical national reports.

The committees publish "general comments" on the states' reports and "general recommendations" which are meant to help states in their *interpretation* of the rights contained in the treaties. The "recommendations" "clarify" the treaty provisions by specifying the actions which the states, groups and individuals should undertake. They may also define standards and suggest actions to protect or "enlarge" a right. The committees also receive complaints from individuals who believe that their rights have been infringed by a state. It is now standard practice for NGOs to submit *shadow reports* to committees. These are reports written by NGOs which have no formal juridical value, but which nevertheless have a strong influence on the experts' decisions regarding states. The treaty monitoring bodies' mechanisms allow the "experts", themselves influenced by sexual and reproductive rights activists, to push states towards interpreting certain rights in such a way as to include sexual and reproductive rights. This mechanism lends itself easily to manipulation. The UN and UNFPA in particular, consider that the consensus of Cairo and Beijing, though not juridically binding, can *inform* the work of the monitoring bodies, and that these should be inspired by the consensus in formulating their recommendations, establishing their standards and interpreting the treaties.

Such was the meaning of the initiative organized at Glen Cove (New York, USA) by UNFPA, the *United Nations High Commissioner for Human Rights* (UNHCHR) and the *Division for the Advancement of Women* (DAW) in 1996. These UN organs gathered members of six treaty monitoring bodies[13] with UN organs and militant sexual and reproductive rights NGOs, to see how to interpret certain fundamental rights so as to ensure that signatory states would enforce sexual and reproductive rights. It was the first time that such a meeting took place. Glen Cove built a bridge between the "experts" of treaty monitoring bodies and reproductive health "experts". From then on, behind the scenes, the latter have been exerting an influence over the monitoring bodies and the interpretation of treaties that seems to have never stopped growing. The monitoring bodies' experts who participated in the Glen Cove meeting, chosen in function of their ideological orientation, declared that "gender equality" (a concept which, we repeat, includes reproductive rights) from then clearly belonged to their respective mandates. They began to integrate sexual and reproductive rights into their work, to give the right to health a gender perspective, to interpret the norms of international treaties in such a way that sexual and reproductive rights were an integral part of the rights contained in the treaties.

Five years after the Glen Cove meeting, in June 2001, UNFPA and UNHCHR organized a follow-up in Geneva. The conclusions of the Geneva meeting were based on the work of experts who had analyzed the manner in which the treaty monitoring bodies were dealing with sexual and reproductive health. These experts put particular emphasis on three issues: "unsafe" abortion, adolescents' access to sexual and reproductive health, and AIDS. In other words, the most controversial and critical issues for the future of humanity are precisely those which the experts would want to integrate without debate or opposition in international law. Their position is explicit. According to the treaties, they say, states have *positive obligations* to implement laws, policies and national programs in such a way as to promote sexual and reproductive health in their countries, and *negative obligations* - namely removing the obstacles to its realization.

To pressure states to accomplish these alleged "obligations", the experts have devised multiple strategies. They prepare, for example, analyses "clarifying" the relation allegedly existing between sexual and reproductive rights and human rights treaties. They disseminate these analyses widely. They encourage treaty monitoring bodies to ask regularly and formally for information from specialized UN agencies in order to know the situation of such or such country in matters of sexual and reproductive health. They place their ideological allies in monitoring bodies. They encourage the creation of NGO coalitions working in the domain of reproductive health so that they can supply monitoring bodies with more complete information. They push NGOs to study, article by article, the human rights treaties to demonstrate that sexual and reproductive rights are indivisible from and interdependent with human rights. They encourage these NGOs to give states directives which they can use when they draft their reports and to report sexual and reproductive rights "violations" to the monitoring bodies. Finally, they expect NGOs to monitor the conclusions drawn by treaty monitoring bodies and make sure that they are effectively implemented.

For its part, UNFPA encourages NGOs to organize political and media campaigns demanding a change in the law where they consider it necessary. NGOs which specialize in reproductive rights" are supposed to train human rights NGOs (such as *Amnesty International*), so that these integrate reproductive rights into their interpretation of rights. UNFPA encourages these NGOs to transfer their "expertise" to an ever growing range of civil society actors.

Treaty monitoring bodies have already made significant progress in the implementation of reproductive rights. In 1999, for example, the *Committee for the Elimination of All Forms of Discrimination against Women* adopted a general recommendation on article 12 of the *Convention*, affirming *inter alia* that member states should ensure universal access for all women to a full and affordable range of quality health care, including sexual and reproductive health care. The *Committee on Children's Rights* concentrated particularly on the issue of the sexual and reproductive rights of children when it studied the right of children to obtain advice and medical treatment "according to their age and maturity", without the need for parental consent. The *Committee on Economic, Social and Cultural Rights* in its fourteenth general commentary on the right to higher standards of health, drawn up in 2000, mentions sexual and reproductive services. The *Human Rights Committee*[14], in its general commentary number 28 on equality, points out that states had no choice but to respect the privacy of women "where there is a requirement for the husband's authorization to make a decision in regard to sterilization..., or where States impose a legal duty upon doctors and other health personnel to report cases of women who have undergone abortion." This committee recommends that states parties "should give information on any measures taken by the State to help women prevent unwanted pregnancies, and to ensure that they do not have to undertake life-threatening clandestine abortions."[15] In reality, committees' recommendations in favor or reproductive rights abound. They particularly insist on the obligations states have to make contraception available to all women, to reinforce sex education programs in schools, to criminalize "marital rape", to liberalize laws authorizing abortion, to combat gender stereotypes, to give adolescents access to reproductive health information without parental knowledge or consent.

WHO was requested to create health indicators which would be used to monitor the implementation of the right to health. WHO's *Department of Reproductive Health and Research* ensures that treaty monitoring bodies address sexual and reproductive health. It organizes briefings for these bodies on trends and indicators in sexual and reproductive health. At the European level, reproductive rights activists believe that the jurisprudence of the *European Commission* and the *European Court of Human Rights* has recognized that articles 2, 3, 8 and 10 of the *European Convention on Human Rights and Fundamental Freedoms* protect reproductive rights.

These developments suggest several observations. First, it is worth noting that a few experts hold an effective global power which is not directly controlled by the elected. They exercize this power not only on treaty monitoring bodies but also on the UN system as a whole, on NGOs, on global civil society, on regional organizations such as the *African Union*, in brief on global governance mechanisms both in the political domain (at the legislative, executive and juridical levels) and in the cultural domain.

Secondly, it is undeniable that among human rights activists, those who militate for sexual and reproductive rights and other rights connected with the "right to choose" have been the most proactive and aggressive. The monitoring mechanisms that they have established to ensure the enforcement of these rights are such that we could end up arriving at a situation where sexual and reproductive rights would be better applied and respected than fundamental human rights. In addition, universal human rights as a whole risk being reinterpreted according to the ideological criteria of the anthropology underlying the "right to choose".

Thirdly, one should be aware that the current reinterpretation of treaties in the light of the new global "consensus" is being carried out in the context of projects to reform the treaty system as a whole. In his September 2002 report on the reform of the UN "Strengthening of the United Nations: an Agenda for Further Change", Kofi Annan advocated the harmonization of the treaty system. He proposed to the monitoring bodies to create a more coordinated approach of their activities and to standardize the demands made on states for the writing of their reports. The *Secretary General* also suggested allowing each state to produce a single report summing up its adherence to all the treaties it had ratified. Because of the pressures exerted by the reproductive rights activists in each monitoring body, reproductive health has become a rallying point for the experts of the different bodies. The integration of reproductive rights risks being given priority in the harmonization process. The possibility of such a development should be monitored with the utmost care.

Finally, if many rejoiced at the creation of the *Human Rights Council*, supposed to reinforce the UN's capacity to promote and to monitor the implementation of human rights, it is important to monitor the way in which the UN machinery interprets the *content* of human rights. If human rights become the instrument with which to apply an ambivalent or radical anthropology, the *Council* would risk lending its institution to subversive or even dictatorial goals.

The Maputo Protocol

On July 11, 2003, at the second ordinary session of the *African Union*, the member states of this regional organization adopted a *Protocol on the Rights of Women in Africa*. Under the pressure of western lobbies which had by then seized power at the level of the *African Union*, the protocol incorporates the ideological objectives of Cairo and Beijing and in particular the right to abortion. Its article 14, "right to health and to control of reproductive functions", stipulates that states which have ratified the protocol are held to "protect the reproductive rights of women, by authorizing medical abortion in cases of of sexual assault, rape, incest and where the continued pregnancy endangers the mental and physical health of the mother or the life of the mother or the foetus." This formula makes the Maputo protocol the juridical instrument that is the most favorable to abortion rights in the world.

As of July 2019, 42 countries out of the 55 member countries of the African Union had ratified the protocol. African populations have not been consulted and to this day still do not realize what has taken place. Once again it is the minorities in power at the level of global governance who have hijacked democracy, the rule of law and human rights even before they could start properly developing on the continent, imposing an agenda which is as contrary to basic African values as it is to universal values. These pressure groups, largely western, are now working to "sensitize" the African public (through the media, the distribution of information on the protocol to governments, judges, lawyers, law students and politicians) about what they call "women's rights" - namely reproductive rights and the right to abortion - and "state obligations". They also seek to "train" those who play a role in the protection, promotion and defense of "women's rights".

Campaigns targeting youth

The Cairo conference insisted with unprecedented force on the sexual and reproductive rights of *adolescents* (10 - 19 years)[16]. The number of young people in that age range today - 1.7 billion - is the largest that the history of humanity has ever known. Since Cairo, the agents of the global erotic revolution have made it their priority goal to establish a *direct partnership* with young people. They teach them to become *aware* of their sexual and reproductive rights and to claim them actively. Their goal is to arrive at access to sexual and reproductive health and rights for *all* young people. The social engineers also mobilize youth, pushing them to unite in a broad campaign in favor of full enjoyment of sexual freedom and the acquisition of autonomous decision-making. They foster an action-centered revolutionary movement founded on the recognition of sexual pleasure as a *right*. The seriousness of this development and of its consequences for the future of the world and of young people can hardly be exaggerated.

The campaign is above all horizontal: addressed to young people and targeted at young people. It co-opts young people directly, forming a youth leadership. Young people themselves become the agents transforming the mentalities and behaviors of other young people - one of the most perverse aspects of the campaign. The social engineers teach young people to persuade their *peers* to use sexual and reproductive health services, to fight to get their ideas accepted, to exert pressure on political institutions up to the highest level. They invite young people to play a direct role in the elaboration of programs which affect them, for example in campaigns for "sexual diversity" and the "morning after pill", and to evaluate for themselves the sexual health services, educational materials and programs targeted at them.

The activists generally define young people's sexual and reproductive rights as "rights" to *complete* sexual and reproductive health - independently of sex, social or juridical status, religion, skin color, sexual orientation or the mental or physical capacity of these young people. By "complete sexual and reproductive health" they understand the right of young people to *be themselves*, to be free to make "their own decisions", to feel good about themselves, their bodies and their sexuality, to express themselves, to enjoy sexual relations, to be active citizens, to have confidence in themselves and their sexuality, to be safe, to choose to marry or not to marry and to plan a family, to *know* (sex, contraceptives, methods for preventing sexually transmissible illnesses and AIDS, their rights), to abort where abortion is legal, to form their own opinions about sexuality, to have access to complete didactic information on sexual and reproductive issues without feeling judged or being made ill at ease, to *protect themselves* and to be protected (from unplanned pregnancies, sexually transmissible illnesses, AIDS and sexual abuse), to have health care which is confidential, affordable, quality and "delivered with respect", and the right to be involved in planning programs with and for young people, to take part in meetings and seminars at all levels and to influence governments by "appropriate means" (*Youth Parliaments*, participation of young people in politics and so on). Certain particularly powerful organizations militate openly for the right of adolescents to have access to "safe" and legal abortion, and they exercise pressure on governments so that they remove all barriers to abortion services for teenagers.

To enforce the "reproductive rights" of young people, the promoters of these rights chiefly use the *Convention on the Rights of the Child*[17], which defines a child as any individual below 18 years of age. This convention recognizes the primacy of the child's interests in family decisions, legal systems and other actions of the state. It also recognizes the "child's evolutive capacity". Driven by an individualistic mentality, the lobbies use this article to spur governments to recognize that the role of parents is limited by the capacity of the child to make "reasonable and independent" decisions. They treat the child chiefly as a *citizen* and not as a member of a *family*. In other words, if a twelve-year old child, for example, is believed to be capable of making an autonomous decision, this child has a right to sexual relations of his or her choice. The lobbies also argue that parents should be "realistic" regarding the sexual activity of their children, and that it is the parents' duty to give their children access to the information necessary for avoiding unwanted pregnancies, sexually transmitted illnesses, AIDS, death and violence. Adolescents' right to confidentiality and privacy is inviolable for these pressure groups.

---

[1] The classic error has been to start acting when the radical agenda threatened to integrate national legislations or international law, in other words downstream of the revolutionary process, while the process should have been monitored upstream.

[2] Cf. the Perruche ruling in France, 17 November 2000.

[3] Implication: they also comprise others.

[4] At Beijing, the homosexual lobby tried to have them formally recognized in the final document but this goal was not achieved.

[5] Such as the *Convention on Civil and Political Rights*, the *Convention on Economic, Social and Cultural Rights*, the *Convention on all Forms of Discrimination against Women*.

[6] See IPPF Charter on Sexual and Reproductive Rights. Guidelines. IPPF.

[7] The global culture has redefined the dignity of the human person: what opposes the freedom to choose has become contrary to dignity. Suffering is also considered contrary to human dignity.

[8] These alleged "violations" could not exist since, as we have said, sexual and reproductive rights have not been included in international law.

[9] A section on reproductive rights was established by the *Office of the High Commission for Human Rights* (OHCHR) in its women's rights department.

[10] Socioeconomic rights, according to the militants, were neglected during the cold war. It was due time, at the end of the cold war, to give them the same importance as that already enjoyed by civil and political rights.

[11] In 1979, the *General Assembly* of the *United Nations* adopted the *Convention on the Elimination of All Forms of Discrimination Against Women* (CEDAW), considered as the "Charter" of Women's Rights. It is the main juridical instrument used by feminists in their attempts to enforce their interpretation of women's rights. This convention, which came into force in 1981, has now been ratified by 180 countries. The Convention has been translated into regional contexts, as for example in the *Convention de Belem do Para* and the *Charte Africaine des Droits Humains et des Personnes* ("African Charter on Human and People's Rights").

[12] There exist more than 80 human rights treaties and declarations.

[13] Namely: *Human Rights Committee; Committee on Economic, Social and Cultural Rights; Committee on the Elimination of Racial Discrimination; Committee against Torture; Committee on the Elimination of Discrimination against Women; Committee on the Rights of the Child.*

[14] Monitoring body of the 1966 *Covenant on Civil and Political Rights*.

[15] See Women's Rights are Human Rights - Reproductive Rights. OHCHR website.

[16] According to the UN, an adolescent is any person between 10 and 19, and young people are those between 10 and 24. For the UN, youth comprises the group of people between 15 and 24.

[17] This convention concerns all children and young people below 18. It is ratified by all countries in the world except the USA and Somalia.

THE HISTORICAL AND INSTITUTIONAL JOURNEY OF THE GLOBALIZATION OF THE REVOLUTION

This chapter traces in broad outline the historical and institutional journey of the globalization of the western erotic revolution since the 1970s. It also identifies the mechanisms of partnerships to which this globalization process owes its effectiveness, and which were transformed, in the course of the 1990s, into *operational networks of normative global governance*, in parallel with traditional intergovernmental multilateralism.

The globalization of the western sexual revolution came about by stages. The "spearhead"[1] individuals were at the origin of *movements* which rapidly organized themselves into pressure groups, NGOs, institutes, foundations and international federations of associations, such as the *International Planned Parenthood Federation* (IPPF), the *International Union for the Scientific Study of Population* (IUSSP), *Marie Stopes International*, the *Population Council*, the *Population Institute*, among many others (see annex B).

When a *critical mass* chooses to swing to the side of the claims of radical minorities and to adopt their ideas, "values", mentalities, behaviors and lifestyles, the revolution is accomplished. Such is today's situation: a critical mass of individuals within local communities have turned against their own traditions to claim as their own the agenda of the agents of global social transformation. Let us note, however, that revolutionary radicalism loses its intensity as it integrates the mass culture. It ends up destructing itself.

In this chapter we shall lastly show that the history of the globalization of the cultural revolution is in large part that of the *integration* of two objectives which have become increasingly interdependent in the socioeconomic policies of international organizations since the 1970s:

the *hedonistic objectives* of the agents of the western sexual revolution, and the *geopolitical interests* of the population control lobby. These two objectives have progressively converged to the point of merging into one at the 1994 Cairo conference.

The role of the IPPF - UN partnership

The history of the partnership which the IPPF forged with the *United Nations* (UN) since the 1960s occupies a particular place in the history of the globalization of the erotic revolution. Founded by Margaret Sanger, the IPPF is a federation today comprising some 150 family planning associations established in more than 180 countries. The IPPF imposes itself as the incontrovertible global *expert* on "sexual and reproductive health" issues and as such exerts immeasurable global influence. Radically permissive, militating for a fundamental right to "safe" abortion and for the "celebration" of "sexual diversity", the IPPF is at once a *pressure group* (operating at the international, regional, national, and local levels) and a *service provider*. The federation also presents itself as an *uncontested defender of human rights*, as we have seen in chapter four.

Since its creation in Bombay in 1952, the federation has had an internationalist perspective which prompted it to work with the UN to try and direct multilateral policies and to maximize its possibilities of influence in the world. The obvious ideological affinities of the UN *Secretariat* with the IPPF explain the solidity of the partnership from the start. In 1964, the IPPF gained consultative status with the *Economic and Social Council* (ECOSOC), in 1965 with the *International Labor Organization* (ILO) and the *United Nations Children's Fund* (UNICEF), in 1966 with the *World Health Organization* (WHO), in 1968 with the *United Nations Educational, Scientific and Cultural Organization* (UNESCO) and the *Food and Agriculture Organization of the United Nations* (FAO). In other words, in just four years' time, the IPPF assured itself a privileged consultative position with the main institutions of international socioeconomic governance.

One year after the May 1968 youth revolt, the UN created the *United Nations Fund for Population Activities* (UNFPA). At the time, the main raison d'être of UNFPA was to reduce demographic growth in developing countries. The creation of a UN structure concerned with issues which the IPPF considered itself expert in, and which disposed of an NGOs liaison section from the 1970s, offered the federation a springboard. From the start, there existed an ideological convergence between the IPPF and the UN. Between 1970 and 1990 the partnership consolidated steadily. In the shadow of the cold war and the nuclear threat then occupying the minds of western political leaders, NGOs militating for "sexual liberation" silently hijacked international organizations. By 1990, individuals belonging to these networks occupied the key strategic positions at the UN. In practice, divergent viewpoints on population issues no longer were no longer allowed at the level of global governance.

The role of the UN conference process from 1968

It was chiefly through the intergovernmental conference process of the UN, which began in 1968 with the Tehran human rights conference, that the western revolutionary agenda progressively internationalized itself. The history of these UN conferences reveals the driving role of western lobbies, which pushed governments to integrate population and women's issues into the activities of the UN. Western minorities successfully used the socioeconomic mandate of the UN, an intergovernmental organization, to impose their non-governmental ideological agendas on UN member states.

A series of UN conferences on population and women took place from the 1970s: on population, in Bucharest in 1974, in Mexico (1984) and in Cairo (1994); on women, in Mexico (1975), Copenhagen (1980), Nairobi (1985) and Beijing (1995). The process of these conferences was launched in the context of the western cultural revolution, a relatively short time after the commercialization of contraception, and at a moment when the rapid acceleration of global population growth particularly excited the lobby militating for the control of the population of poor countries. This historical context explains the ease with which radical pressure groups were able to hijack UN conferences and impose their views and policies on the governments of developing countries during the cold war.

The preparations for a UN intergovernmental conference demand an effort to mobilize national delegations. They go through a "consensus-building" process which, as we shall see in chapter six, has been one of the main manipulation methods used by revolutionary agents to rally the greatest possible number of governments to their aganda. The practice of "consensus-building" has evolved at the UN. At Bucharest, voting - which allows clear expression of one's opposition to UN proposals - was still much in use. In Mexico in 1984, voting was strongly reduced, to be finally totally abandoned at Cairo. *Consensus* has now become a norm of global governance and an imperative of the new postmodern ethic.

Note in addition that the preparatory process of an intergovernmental conference demands on the part of the UN an *internal* coordination effort. The conferences have thereby contributed to the progressive unification of the UN system, since the 1970s, around the objectives of the conferences and those of the lobbies which have infiltrated them - objectives which have ended up surreptitiously transforming the organization's mandate from within.

The integration process: from the sectorial approach of the 1970s to the holistic approach of the 1990s

During the years 1960-70, human rights, the environment, socioeconomic development, food, work, culture, education, health, security and peace were understood, at the international as well as the national levels, as separate domains: the approach was *sectorial*. When one wished to draw the attention of governments to a new issue, such as women or population, one created, respectively, *Ministries of Women's Affairs* and *Family Planning Units* in national administrative structures, often within *Finance* or *Ministries of Planning*. The aim of creating these new structures was to breach the institutional body so as to give visibility to the objectives one was pursuing. Nevertheless, the sectorial approach was but a stage in the pursuit of a strategic plan with holistic ambitions.

The agitators' plan was in effect to progressively link the different domains of socioeconomic development among themselves so as to make them definitively interdependent within a new ethical system governed by their own values and ideological priorities. To build this system, the lobbies promoted the creation of "linkages" between domains which, by their very nature, were distinct. Hence they integrated into development policies: family planning, gender equality, population stabilization, women's rights and the transformation of mentalities - along with the deconstruction of traditional values which is implied in the way they interpret these objectives. Minority interest groups strove to hide their subversive intentions in a new system which externally appeared neutral as a whole.

To gain a critical mass to their vision, the population control lobbies used subtle propaganda forms. Having indoctrinated the masses about the alleged threat of "overpopulation" of the planet, they strove to "prove" its link with risks of famine, the rise of poverty, the general deterioration of "quality of life", the extinction of species and the "depletion" of natural resources[2] - all to the end of gaining acceptance for the *absolute priority* which they wanted to give to population control objectives in international development programs. The message was the following: if poor countries want to develop, they must *start* by controlling their population. In other words, to eliminate poverty, you must start by eliminating the poor.

According to the logic of the agents of social transformation, population control had to be at the heart of food security policies, socio-economic development, environmental protection and a new ethic of "quality of life for all". It was also necessary to link economic development to the empowerment of women and their rights, and to link these to free access to contraception and "safe" abortion. These *artificial linkages* clashed with traditional values and necessitated a radical change of mentalities and cultures. Finally and fundamentally, it was necessary to link ideology to *education*, and to use education to propagate ideology.

For the militants of the global cultural revolution, the challenge of the great international conferences of the UN was to successfully achieve the process of integration as we have just described it: governments would thereby rally to their agenda without even being aware of it. The success of the integration strategy proved immeasurable: the *holistic vision* of the agents of transformation succeeded, over some thirty years' time, in imposing itself into multilateral forums to the extent of becoming the object of a global consensus at the end of the cold war, as we have seen in chapter two. At the start of the 1990s, human rights, socioeconomic development, the promotion of women, population issues, environmental protection, peace, had become interdependent themes within a new global ethical framework. The "new world order" of the 1990s is the result of a process of integration going back to the 1970s.

The integration process took place in a series of successive steps. As already mentioned, the challenge of the process was to end up in a dialectical synthesis of the *individualistic* objectives of the western sexual revolution (pleasure-seeking, free choice) and the *collectivistic* objectives of the population control lobby (international security, socioeconomic development, environmental protection, human security), to reach a *balance* between individual well-being and planetary survival.

Individualism and collectivism seem incompatible: the first promotes absolute individual *freedom*, while the second passes via *constraint* to give societies the number of children which the state, or a "higher" instance such as the *World Bank* or the UN, believes they need: the individual is then conditioned so as to conform his individual behavior to collective "obligations". However, the two movements join in their anti-conception mentality, their will to assure individuals free access to contraception and "safe" abortion.

The conferences of the UN aimed to progressively transform mentalities in such a way that the collectivist objectives could be achieved not by force but by what would pass for the exercise of the "right to choose" of the individual. Hence these conferences surfed on the cultural revolution which has transformed mores, restructured society, destabilized the traditional family, promoted alternative family structures (homosexuality, homosexual parenting…), changed lifestyles and sexual practices. Once mentalities were transformed, individuals would no longer be inclined to "choose" anything but the agenda of the revolution. In the final analysis, the "right to choose" was supposed to mean mainly the "right not to have children".

Experience has taught the anti-natalist lobbies that the promotion of contraception in developing countries does not guarantee that women will use it. The "encouragements" and "discouragements" given by the governments of developing countries to their populations to reduce fertility or rates of demographic growth did not produce the expected results. A change of strategy was needed. Let us repeat, it was by unleashing the feminist and erotic revolution in these countries that lobbies thought to control their population more effectively and rapidly.

The great UN conferences of the 1990s marked the final and historic stage of integration. The platform for action of the Rio conference (1992), *Agenda 21*, for example, underscored the *synergistic relation* which existed between demographic trends and "sustainable development"[3], a concept which, as we have seen, *integrates* economic development, social equity and environmental protection. The Cairo platform for action espoused an *integrated vision*, according to which reproductive health cannot progress outside the context of a wider social change, within the framework of sustainable development and good governance (partnerships with NGOs) and above all of the new ethic of *free choice*. Demographic stabilization now only goes through the exercise of sexual and reproductive rights, and population policies are *integrated* into sustainable development programs - since demographic growth allegedly accelerates certain environmental degradation processes. The "population units" created from the 1970s have no further purpose: population factors are now supposed to be fully *integrated* into the perspectives of all the ministries linked with socioeconomic development, including environment ministries.

We have seen how the Cairo perspective is *holistic*. The Cairo consensus integrates demographic objectives into a new system indissolubly linking population stabilization, poverty reduction, economic progress, environmental protection, reduction of production and consumption levels, gender equality, universal access to primary education, empowerment of women, intergenerational equity, reduction of infant, child and maternal mortality, development of human resources, opposition to all forms of constraint, protection of vulnerable groups and sexual and reproductive health. Holism is the result of an integration process carried out since the 1960s by the agents of cultural transformation.

The "population question"

From the end of the Second World War, the world's population increased at the unprecedented rate of two percent annually. In 1950 it passed the two and a half billion mark, and was six billion by the turn of the century. This growth rate slowed down during the 1980s. The population control agitprop started to make itself heard in the 1950s. In 1954, the American Hugh Moore circulated a pamphlet entitled *The Population Bomb*. In 1968 Paul Ehrlich, a professor at *Stanford University*, published a book with the same title which became massively influential. In 1972, Donella and Dennis Meadows submitted to the *Club of Rome*[4] a plea in favor of halting population growth entitled *The Limits to Growth*. Their report set out to show the "dramatic" social and environmental consequences of the exponentially increasing consumption of resources which it stressed were "limited". It concluded that if this rate was sustained, the limits to growth would be reached towards the middle of the 21st century.

The hypothesis of a population explosion formulated by "experts" in the 1950s and 60s gave rise to campaigns waving the spectre of imminent famines and alarming environmental degradation, and exhorting governments and the "international community" to apply draconian population control policies in developing countries. The three UN population conferences (Bucharest 1974, Mexico 1984, and Cairo 1994) studied demographic trends based on the statistics of the *Population Division* of the UN *Secretariat*. In fact, global population growth has slowed at a rate greater than anticipated by the forecasts on which the policies of these three conferences were based. Notwithstanding, the population control lobby continued to believe that annual demographic growth in terms of absolute figures remained alarming[5] and that this growth justified perseverance in the struggle for demographic control. The Cairo program of action pursued the objective of facilitating *demographic transition* - the transition from high birth and death rates to lower ones - as quickly as possible throughout the world. Cairo affirmed that such a transition would contribute to the *stabilization of world population*[6]. Of course, population control policies are targeted at developing countries with the highest growth rate (2.7%, for example, in Africa, while it is 0.4% in the West).

The NSSM 200 or "Kissinger report"

In 1974, the year when the first UN population conference took place, the *National Security Council* of the United States produced, under the direction of Henry Kissinger, then *Secretary of State*, an internal study entitled *Implications of Worldwide Population Growth for U.S. Security and Overseas Interests*[7], also known as *Memorandum 200* or *NSSM 200*. The message of the report, made public in 1989, was that the demographic growth of developing countries was susceptible to becoming a security problem for America: a source of social destabilization, and thus a threat to the supply of the resources necessary for the American economy. By linking *security* and *population control*, the Kissinger report led the *integration process* we have spoken of a step further.

The authors of the *Memorandum* recommended to the American administration, in order "to minimize charges of an imperialist motivation behind its support of population activities" to repeatedly assert "that such support derives from a concern with: a) the right of the individual to determine freely and responsibly the number and spacing of children... and b) the fundamental social and economic development of poor countries"[8]. Consequently, since 1974, the population control strategy has been going through a reinterpretation of fundamental human rights and the transformation of mentalities in favor of the "right to choose".

From then on, demographic control through family planning has become a priority objective of American foreign policy and of the West in general. The pursuit of this objective was relatively cheap with respect to the strategic effectiveness it ensured. To respond to the criticisms which it drew, pointing out that western aid to health programs in developing countries was diminishing while population control funding was increasing, population programs were integrated into health programs (particularly into maternal health programs): expenditures for demographic control were merged into the budget for health expenditures[9]. The *population control - maternal health* link was created, reinforcing the integration process.

Bucharest 1974

Let us now return to the survey of the process of the UN conferences on population, starting with the 1974 Bucharest conference. Before Bucharest, the UN had already organized, with the *International Union for the Scientific Study of population* (IUSSP)[10], two "scientific" meetings, in Rome in 1954 and Belgrade in 1965, where the relation between demographic growth and socioeconomic development was studied. These meetings were directed so as to "prove" that "overpopulation" harmed economic development. Rome and Bucharest were not intergovernmental conferences, but meetings of experts. The viewpoint of these "experts" has nevertheless had a critical influence on the content of the intergovernmental conference of Bucharest, whose final plan invited countries to adopt population policies into the framework of socioeconomic development: one of the first stages of the integration process.

Let us repeat, "experts" have piloted governments from behind the scenes since the first UN intergovernmental conferences. A breakdown in democracy compromised the legitimacy and authenticity of the process of the great UN conferences from its origins.

At Bucharest, the viewpoint of the West and Asia was that rapid demographic growth in a given country intensified its socioeconomic problems. Bangladesh, India and Indonesia supported the family planning programs proposed by the West. On the other hand, African and

Southern American countries were strongly opposed to demographic control and did not want to integrate them into development. The delegations of these countries expressed clearly what developing countries wanted: growth, not demographic control. Faced by this opposition, the western lobbies had to refine their strategy. They did so by insisting increasingly on the *individual rights* approach - which they radically reinterpreted in the light of their ideology - and on the link between population control and economic development.

It is necessary in this chapter on the history of the globalization of the revolution to recall that the Bucharest conference[11] eliminated the word *parents* from multilateral language, and recognized the fundamental right of all *couples* and *individuals* to decide in a free and responsible manner the number and spacing of their children and to have the information, education and means to do so. From then on, the "international community" accepted that contraceptives should be made available to non-married individuals. Bucharest had integrated not only population and development, but also the idea that human rights transcend sovereignty - an idea that those lobbying for the "right to choose" (including to have an abortion) did not fail to exploit abundantly thereafter.

We note that already at Bucharest, members of the IPPF were part of some national delegations, particularly Asian and European ones. Since Bucharest, individuals of IPPF's ideological tendency have taken the initiative to create "caucuses" or "informal committees" parallel to the intergovernmental process to negotiate compromise solutions to "hard questions"[12]. It is by this kind of procedure that the ideas of the western sexual revolution became integrated into global governance.

CONGO, the association of NGOs accredited to ECOSOC, had created a committee to organize NGO activity in parallel with the intergovernmental conference of Bucharest (the *Population Tribune*)[13]. We note that the final document of Bucharest only mentions NGOs in a subsidiary way, underlining the major role of governments. At the time, many governments of developing countries viewed NGOs with a certain distrust, accusing them of reflecting western interests. Since Bucharest, however, the number of NGOs devoted to population, development, women and the environment has continued to increase substantially. These NGOs began to receive funding from governmental and non governmental sources, and were increasingly recognized by the UN[14].

The manner in which governments of developing countries grasp issues of demographic growth rates and fertility levels has changed dramatically since the Bucharest conference. Among the nine most populated countries (Bangladesh, India, Indonesia, Pakistan, China, Egypt, Nigeria, Mexico and Brazil), only the first four had birth control policies in 1974. Ten years later at the Mexico conference, China, Nigeria and Brazil had changed their position in favor of a lowered growth rate, and more than 25 African countries had pronounced themselves on the "urgency" of demographic questions[15].

Mexico 1984

The Mexico conference marked, under President Reagan, a radical change in American population policy. The United States would no longer consider demographic growth as an unfavorable economic factor, but as a "neutral" factor. The US delegation to Mexico, led by James Buckley, achieved the adoption of a policy according to which America would no longer finance population activities which included abortion: the "Mexico City Policy". The United States withdrew their voluntary contribution to the IPPF in 1985 and to UNFPA in 1986.

By contradistinction, China changed policy at Mexico and became favorable to population reduction measures; ten years earlier at Bucharest, China believed that demographic growth was necessary for the purposes of military defense. India, Pakistan, Bangladesh and Indonesia continued to strongly support the UN's demographic control objectives. Nigeria, Kenya and other African countries, which had been reticent at Bucharest, evolved at Mexico in the direction of the UN. In a general sense, the western population control lobby believed that the Mexico conference revealed a greater support from developing countries for anti-natalist objectives. This calls for a comment. The "support" of developing countries for UN policies was neither free nor authentic: it was given under the pressure of the anti-natalist lobby's economic blackmail, according to which these countries would not benefit from development aid as long as they did not implement the demographic control policies in conformity with UN objectives.

The Mexico conference strongly encouraged governments to ensure adequate financial resources to family planning. While the Bucharest approach was more theoretical than operational, Mexico approved concrete recommendations. The conference introduced the idea of the information needs of teenagers, of the importance of men's role in planning and of the role and status of women: these themes would become of central importance at Cairo, ten years later.

The Mexico conference also revealed the rise in the influence of family planning NGOs and the experience they had gained. An NGO forum took place in Geneva a few months prior to Mexico. The Mexico document stimulated NGOs to continue their "pioneering work in opening new paths" for the implementation of the conference's platform for action[16]. Mexico encouraged the "innovative" character, the "experience" and the "expertise" of NGOs.

Privileged working relationships, culminating in the formulation of common interests and objectives, were gradually established between UN officials and an increasing variety of feminist and family planning NGOs. As these relations grew in strength, the UN steadily encouraged and reinforced its partnership with NGOs. This partnership developed *in parallel* with the intergovernmental process, without ever being seriously submitted to the control of governments. A divorce within the UN ensued from this situation: the *Secretariat* (collaborating on the content of international policies directly, but by stealth, with NGOs) ceased to behave primarily as the "secretary" of UN member states and became increasingly autonomous from intergovernmental mechanisms. But the common strategic interests of the UN-NGO partnership have, in the majority of cases, nothing to do with the real interests of developing countries.

The Amsterdam forum

UNFPA celebrated its twentieth anniversary in 1989 and organized an *International Population Forum* in Amsterdam on this occasion. Numerous NGOs took part in the event. The *Amsterdam Declaration* set the framework for UNFPA's future strategy: increase in the use of contraceptives in developing countries, to reach 56% of women of childbearing age before the year 2000; reduction of women's fertility rate; a doubling of investments in population programs in the developing countries.

Mexico, Copenhagen, Nairobi, Beijing

One year after Bucharest, on the occasion of international women's year, in 1975, the UN organized a conference on women in Mexico, which was followed by the UN women's decade (1976 - 1985). Three intergovernmental conferences on women followed on from the Mexico conference: Copenhagen (1980), Nairobi (1985) and finally Beijing (1995). The women's conferences of Mexico (1975) and Copenhagen (1980) had "sensitized" the international community and generated much public attention on women's issues. However, the intergovernmental women's conference process was itself rapidly hijacked by radical pressure groups.

The Mexico document still mentioned the fulfilment of women in their *family* role and the importance of sustaining their social role as *mothers*. But at the initiative of Nafis Sadik[17] and other agents of the globalization of the feminist and sexual revolution, a women's caucus, consisting of feminist NGOs, was formed in Mexico. The caucus managed to open a separate section on *women's rights*. The Copenhagen conference integrated health and education in its program - the two domains *par excellence* which enacted the drama of the western cultural revolution. The Nairobi conference introduced women's equal rights to divorce, and began to insist much more on so-called "family" planning, thereby integrating population issues into the framework of an intergovernmental women's conference. Nairobi also spoke more openly about the particular role of women in population control processes.

The IPPF's new strategic direction, and the Cairo Copernican turn

In 1992, the IPPF celebrated its fortieth anniversary in New Delhi[18]. The federation recognized that it was at a crossroads. As it wrote in *Vision 2000*, the strategic plan which emerged from the New Delhi meeting, it could either "choose to rest on the laurels of its past success, and continue as before, presuming that it had assured of a leadership position in the family planning movement of the future" or "take stock of its environment by recognizing the challenge of the issues confronting it, and once again become a pioneering organization, adopting causes which others are shy to espouse, seizing opportunities to be innovative, and persevering in its capacity as the voice of the voiceless." The IPPF, which considers itself as "THE conscience and THE leader of the family planning movement in the NGO sector"[19], chose the second option.

The new line traced by the IPPF was that adopted at Cairo. To this day, it remains the line followed by international cooperation: the "unmet needs" approach[20] (of women for contraception, of young people for information, etc.), sexual and reproductive health, "safe abortion"[21], women's empowerment[22], information and services for young people, and "quality" services. The IPPF believed that the small family was becoming the "cultural norm everywhere" and that sexual and reproductive health was "becoming an integral part of the health culture"[23]. The federation wanted, on the one hand, to reduce the high rate of "unsafe" abortions, and on the other to increase the right of access to legal and "safe" abortion.

The analysis brought to New Delhi by Steven Sinding, then *Population Director* at the *Rockefeller Foundation* and later the *General Director* of the IPPF, had a decisive impact on the influence that the IPPF in its turn had on the Cairo document[24]. Sinding proposed abandoning demographic targets. He was convinced, on the basis of his findings, that it would be incomparably more efficient to express the family planning objectives (an expression equally covering, since the Bucharest conference, the "right to choose" of couples and individuals and population control) uniquely in terms of "needs" or "reproductive desires" of women and couples. The concept of "unmet needs" became the IPPF's new catchphrase. At Cairo, numerous governmental delegations, particularly western ones[25], included IPPF representatives.

Let us note that the Cairo conference took place at a time when the myth of overpopulation was collapsing. The UN itself recognized that it had been wrong in its alarmist predictions and began to worry about the depopulation of certain regions of the world, notably Europe. It was no longer strategically possible, at Cairo, to promote "population control" as it had been practised before.

As we have already repeatedly remarked it, the new approach implies that individuals appropriate and internalize the contraceptive and abortive mentality and identify with the principles of the erotic revolution. It necessitates a transformation of mentalities that goes through a combat against traditional values. The greatest achievement of the promoters of sexual and reproductive health and rights at Cairo is without doubt that of having "broken a major taboo" in an intergovernmental forum by provoking a discussion on sexuality which they qualified as "frank and open", which is to say taking place outside any traditional moral framework.

The Cairo revolution was not self-evident; it did not happen without turbulence. The conference was animated by a dramatic atmosphere. For the agents of the global cultural revolution, Cairo was a historic moment. While the conference began "with uncertainties and tensions", it ended, according to them, "in a blaze of glory"[26]. The revolutionaries broadly won the day: the adoption of their "rights approach", which was to bring with it a profound transformation of global public opinion, would in its turn be followed by a universal upheaval in social behavior.

The "partnership principle" between governments and NGOs, between the UN and NGOs, made a decisive advance at Cairo. The Cairo platform for action devoted a whole chapter to the non-governmental sector in which it affirmed that "NGOs should have a key role in national and international development processes"[27]. It is significant that this chapter refers to "partnership" with NGOs (a concept which implies a certain "equality" between the governmental and non-governmental partners), and not simply to collaboration or cooperation between governments and NGOs. Cairo speaks of the *comparative advantage* of NGOs in the implementation of UN policies: NGOs would be more *flexible* than governments, more *innovative*, have a greater *ground experience*, a greater capacity to connect with populations neglected by governments, and a greater *interaction with the grass roots*[28].

4,200 representatives from more than 1,500 NGOs took part in the NGO Forum at Cairo. It is legitimate to affirm that powerful international NGOs have been, even before governments, the first partners of the UN in conceptualizing the objectives of the new global consensus on sexual and reproductive health. Apart from the IPPF, whose paramount influence has already been mentioned, other examples are *Catholics for a Free Choice* founded by Frances Kissling in 1973[29] and the *Women's Environment and Development Organization* (WEDO), created in 1990.

A word is in order about WEDO and its founder, the legendary Bella Abzug, who passed away after the Beijing conference, in 1998. A charismatic and colorful leader of the American eco-feminist movement, militating *inter alia* for lesbian rights, Bella Abzug had been active at the international level since the first conference on women in Mexico in 1975. Upon her initiative, in 1991 WEDO called the *World Women's Congress for a Healthy Planet* in Miami, Florida, gathering some 1,500 women from 83 countries. This congress produced the *Women's Action Agenda 21*, a document which had a major influence on the Beijing conference. Before the 1992 Rio conference, WEDO had launched a *Women's Caucus*, a sort of collective of feminist and libertarian NGOs conceived as a methodology for seizing power at the UN through "civil society". At the UN conferences held between 1992 and 1995, the *Women's Committee* organized a veritable civil society "coup d'etat", imposing its views with incontrovertible force on the intergovernmental process. The *Committee* was one of the most influential lobbies at the great UN conferences of the 1990s. Claiming to represent all the women of the world at the UN, it met daily to plan its strategies. Let us note that Bella Abzug was part of the American delegation to Cairo.

WEDO ensured that the empowerment of women would become the most important *cross-cutting* issue of the Cairo agenda for action. As a consequence of the pressures WEDO exerted on national delegations, the principle of gender equality guided the drafting of the Cairo document and became an issue present in nearly all chapters of the final document. The ground was thus laid for the Beijing conference.

Beijing and *gender*

Cairo turned into a global norm the libertarian ideology conveyed by the IPPF in particular. Beijing globalized the gender feminism ideology proposed by WEDO and other minority groups. The *gender perspective*, warhorse of Bella Abzug, became the central theme of the Beijing conference, notably under the pressure of WEDO[30]. As we have seen it already, since Beijing, all programs, projects, policies and development activities - governmental or non-governmental - have been conceived within the analytical framework of the gender ideology. But the globalization of the feminist revolution was not a foregone conclusion. It required the revolutionary genius of Bella Abzug, who ensured the success of the NGO coup d'etat.

The Cairo and Beijing institutional machinery of implementation

In record time, a gigantic machinery was mobilized after the Cairo and Beijing conferences to globalize the western sexual and feminist revolution. This machinery comprises so many organs that it is impossible to name them all.

The great conferences of the first half of the 1990s were followed by several waves of internal reform at the UN, whose main objective was to align the programs, funds and agencies of the organization with the "new consensus", to make the UN more efficient in the implementation of sustainable development and other objectives of the conferences. It was a matter of reforming the organization in such a way as to apply the new vision through each of its organs according to its particular *comparative advantage*.

A new form of inter-agency cooperation and a redistribution of tasks within the framework of the new consensus started in 1995. As soon as he was named *Secretary General* of the UN in 1996, when the process of the large conferences had just been completed[31], Kofi Annan launched a first wave of organizational reform. Many others followed. The last one was the object of negotiations at the September 2005 summit and is currently being carried out. On January 1st, 2011, a new entity, *UN Women*, became operational.

The UN machinery's unity of action is by now formidable. On issues of reproductive health and gender, the UN speaks with one voice. Not one UN institution remains outside the line set by Cairo and Beijing.

Let us mention, first of all, the institutions most implicated in implementing the Cairo and Beijing agendas: the *United Nations Fund for Population Activities* (UNFPA)[32]; the *World Health Organization* (WHO); the *United Nations Children's Fund* (UNICEF); the *United Nations Development Fund for Women* (UNIFEM)[33]; the UN *Secretariat*, and in particular its *Population Division* (secretariat of the *Commission on Population and Development* dependent on the *Economic and Social Council* or ECOSOC), and its *Division for the Advancement of Women* (DAW, the secretariat of the *Commission on the Status of Women*, also belonging to the ECOSOC system). The UN also has at its disposal a research institute: the *United Nations International Research and Training Institute for the Advancement of Women* (INSTRAW).

In addition, the majority of UN agencies, funds and programs have a department or important programs working on projects concerning women, reproductive health and gender. Such is the case of the *United Nations Development Program* (UNDP), the *United Nations Education, Science and Culture Organization* (UNESCO), the *Joint United Nations Programme on HIV/AIDS* (UNAIDS), the *International Labor Organization* (ILO), the *Office of the United Nations High Commissioner for*

Human Rights, the *World Bank* ("*Gender and Development*" Group), the *Food and Agriculture Organization* (FAO). To this list also belong inter-agency organs, such as the *Inter-agency Task Force on Gender and MDGs*, or the *Millennium Project Task Force on Gender Equality and Education*, the *United Nations Inter-Agency Network on Women and Gender Equality* (IANWGE), to which belong twenty-five organs of the UN, and the *Regional Commissions* of the UN. A large number of these bodies maintain regular and close normative and technical links with certain government ministries (*Foreign Affairs, Health, Development, Planning, Education*) and development cooperation agencies.

If the UN and a handful of NGO partners, as well as the Clinton administration and the *European Union*, have played a driving role in launching the globalization of the western cultural revolution in the first half of the 1990s, the other international organizations rapidly fell into step and integrated the new concepts without debate, out of sheer conformism: among others, the OECD, the G-8, the *Commonwealth* and the *Francophonie* movement. The UN system has been one of the principal *global agents of social transformation* during the first half of the 1990s, the forum in which the consensus was forged. Since then, the revolution decentralized and spread through countless channels, independently from the UN, beyond the UN, and outside the UN, and particularly through the *partnerships regime* we studied in chapter two.

The beginnings of the implementation phase were characterized by an increasingly systemic integration of the concepts within each other and consequently by the reinforcement of the cohesion of the post-modern value system which links them, as well as by the cohesion of the global governance mechanisms geared towards their implementation: reproductive health and gender are no longer only a matter for UN specialized bodies, but also for the whole system - and not only for the UN system, but also for other global governance actors, be they also international organizations or regional ones, national or local authorities, businesses, educational institutions, health services or NGOs.

The implementation phase: from agenda to action

Satisfied with the historical ideological gains obtained in their favor at Cairo and Beijing, the agents of social transformation immediately 126 exerted pressure on governments after the conferences so as to move without delay "from agenda to action" - so that they honor their "commitments" by implementing the objectives of the conferences. The agents of the global cultural revolution did not want to allow governments time to reflect on the content of the consensus, to discover the radical agenda hiding behind the new language, to reopen the alleged consensus and to *backtrack*. At the same time they wished at all costs to protect what they called the "integrity" of the consensus - in other words the inclusion of their non-governmental agenda into the intergovernmental consensus - and to "look forward", to implement the "consensus" as quickly and universally as possible.

In fact, the Cairo and Beijing "consensus", though constructed by minorities at the rudder of global governance (the UN-NGOs alliance), not only were never reopened by governments, but they continued to penetrate ever deeper into the cultures of the world, a great many of which it already imbibes, without meeting major obstacles. Governments and civil societies are now governed by minority ideologues who have prescribed the orientation of these conferences. Political leaders have lacked a clear vision of the issues, moral leadership, political will, courage to correct the drift, sufficient knowledge and the intellectual capacity to formulate an adequate conceptual response. When not complicit, governments lagged behind the UN and NGOs as much when the agenda was set as during the implementation phase, which could have been the occasion to challenge the so-called "consensus". Passive or compromised, the majority behaved as if they were morally bound by a consensus which is not legally binding. In the absence of any decontamination, the situation rotted.

Let us repeat that, juridically speaking, a consensus is not binding upon states. Governments are not obliged to implement the Cairo and Beijing conferences. Nevertheless, the activists of the revolution have constantly recalled governments to the "moral obligation" to respect the "promises" they made at these conferences. They have held them "accountable": "civil society is watching you!" was a favorite slogan of the 1990s. The revolutionary activists counted on the existence of an *intergovernmental* consensus to impose their *non-governmental* interpretation of this same alleged consensus on the ground. By "implementation" they understand a cultural transformation requiring a general mobilization of social actors to make the majority tilt in favor of their own objectives and values. The implementation of global norms concretely translates not only in changes in laws and policies at national levels in the domains of development, health, human rights and gender equality, but above all in a practical transformation of mentalities at the most local level possible: local authorities, schools, dispensaries, families, youth groups, churches, synagogues and mosques, and so on. The social engineers seek to progressively turn their vision into culture. They militate tirelessly to this end. As the implementation of Cairo and Beijing progresses on the ground, they meet with less and less resistance. Already now, they hardly need to struggle: things seem to happen on their own.

"Watchdog" NGOs use highly diversified methods to "monitor" that governments implement Cairo and Beijing. For example, they study governments' budgetary allocations to programs devoted to "gender equality". They pressure governments to produce gender disaggregated statistics. They measure women's participation in political life and their access to power, women's economic autonomy, their employment conditions and the governments' respect for sexual and reproductive rights. In post-conflict situations such as in Afghanistan, Kosovo, Iraq, or numerous African countries, they intervene directly so that new constitutions reflect their values and priorities. They take pains to demonstrate the economic benefits of gender equality as they understand the concept. They constantly complain about the lack of priority governments give to their objectives. They are helped in their efforts by manuals produced by UN agencies, such as the *Resource Guide for Gender Theme Groups* produced jointly by UNIFEM, UNFPA, UNICEF and UNDP in 2005.

The conferences of the 1990s were not conceived as isolated events, but as long-term programs to be applied over an extended time until the anticipated results would be reached. They contain a certain number of concrete recommendations to be applied within a determined time frame. The Cairo document, for example, contains 243 recommendations to be implemented by 2015.

Governmental implementation of the Cairo and Beijing conferences is formally "monitored" once a year by two intergovernmental organs of the UN *Economic and Social Council*: respectively by the *Commission on Population and Development*, and by the *Commission on the Status of Women*. At the annual meetings of these commissions, the social engineers have till now aggressively made sure that governments interpret the consensus in the light of their ideological objectives. To monitor governments' "progress", the UN and NGOs have developed "indicators of progress" and identified the "best practices" governments must follow as examples. Countries have been pressured to submit "implementation reports" to the UN and to prepare national action plans. National implementation has also been "monitored" at the intergovernmental conferences which took place five years after the various "great conferences", called the "plus five": Rio plus five (1997), Cairo plus five (1999), Beijing plus five (2000)...

On the whole, the "plus five" conferences proved a failure for the extremists seeking to further their radicalism. For example, they unsuccessfully demanded that the right to sexual orientation be included in the intergovernmental document of Beijing plus five. Fearing that the Bush administration would provoke a reopening of the debate on the Cairo "gains", the agents of social transformation preferred to cancel plans for Cairo "plus ten" in New-York, and organize more discreet events, at the regional level.

Nevertheless, the follow-up conferences did strengthen the consensus and made definitively impossible to question or reverse it. No one and no government would now contest that the great conferences of the 1990s have provided the international community with the "global agenda" and the "vision" they needed for the 21st century.

The UN and its partners talk of the "mandate" of the great conferences, particularly the "Beijing mandate". The concept of mandate is juridically precise and demanding, but the agents of transformation use it in a fuzzy way. It is by design that they use this word - to reinforce the pseudo "authority" of the consensus and create a pseudo "obligation" to implement it. The consensus, however, has not been the object of a juridical process and would not be able, by the same token, to have the nature of a mandate. Further, governments formally mandated no one at Cairo or Beijing.

Decentralization and localization

The *decentralization* and *localization* processes play an increasingly important role in the implementation of the new global ethic. The consensus forged at the *global* level by a handful of *experts* was, from the start, strategically designed to be implemented at the *local* level by *all the citizens of the world*. Let us make clear that, as the UN conceives it, decentralization concerns only the implementation of global ethical norms - not their formulation. In other words, the UN would not allow intermediate institutions to differentiate themselves from the conceptual framework set up at the global level.

In the framework of the UN reform process, the *United Nations Development Program* (UNDP), the UN body in charge of decentralization, gained and now occupies a central place. In its role as "Resident Coordinator", ensuring the coordination on the ground of the implementation of the great conferences and other UN objectives by different UN bodies in developing countries, the UNDP has been constantly reinforced in recent years.

The decentralization process has two facets: on the one hand, it boosts the responsibility of UN national offices, and on the other, it encourages national authorities to appropriate global norms, and this under the pressure of UN national offices and the resident coordinator.

Let us mention again that the decentralization process increasingly goes through the regional level (organizations such as the *African Union* or the *European Union*) and the local level (local authorities, mayors of towns and villages). As the new paradigms have already been integrated into the policies of a majority of governmental institutions, in the majority of countries, efforts are now centered increasingly on their regional and local implementation. Decentralization and localization render the strategies of global governance agents more and more diffuse, elusive and difficult to control.

It is worth underlining the role played by NGO federations or associations of associations accredited with the UN and aligned on the ideological priorities of the organization. "Umbrella organizations" have proven to be a remarkably efficient bridge in channelling the "global" priorities to the local level, managing to reach even the most decentralized regions. The process of localization takes place without the ordinary citizen's being aware of it: through the Internet, the publications of the umbrella organizations, their policies, their networks of networks, their conferences and training seminars, their activities and local offices. An example is the *World Association of United Cities and Local governments*. The implementation of "gender equality", in the sense that the Beijing conference gave this expression, at the local level of towns, communes and villages is one of the priority objectives of this umbrella organization.

Gender mainstreaming at the UN

To mainstream the *gender perspective* in the reformed UN organization, Kofi Annan named, directly after the Beijing conference, a *Special Adviser on Gender Issues*, to whom he attributed a mandate covering the entire UN system. The office is called the *Office of the Special Adviser on Gender Issues and Advancement of Women*, or OSAGI. The role of OSAGI is to develop methods and tools to facilitate system-wide "gender mainstreaming", and to monitor the "progress" achieved by the different sections of the *Secretariat*, the *Regional Commissions* and the different UN offices throughout the world. It is legitimate to say that *gender mainstreaming* has already been successfully achieved, not only at the UN, but also in all the political, education and health institutions throughout the world.

In a letter addressed to UN agency heads in October 1997, Kofi Annan established that responsibility for *gender mainstreaming* was incumbent on the UN system as a whole, and in particular at the highest level of agencies, departments, funds and commissions: according to the *Secretary General*, the change had to take place within the UN from the top down. Experts had to "educate" senior UN officials[34]. Numerous *gender units* or *gender focal points*, made up of experts, have been created in various strategic points of the UN system so that the global gender specialists can "help" the senior management to "take up their responsibilities", "develop their competencies" by "sensitizing" them, provide them with knowledge and information, and encourage their commitment. This makes it evident that the global normative power of experts has become excessive and goes as far as to threaten, to our mind, the very functioning of democracy.

The principle applied within the UN has extended to the relation of the UN with governments. Bypassing the *General Assembly*, some specialized UN bodies have "helped" (which is to say "pressured") governments bilaterally to develop so-called "gender sensitive" policies, which are in reality those of a minority of experts and feminist activists. The UN has encouraged governments to tackle the issue from the top, in other words starting with the leaders.

Let us give an example of UN institutional changes which have resulted from the implementation of *gender mainstreaming*. Like all UN organizations, WHO integrated the *gender perspective* after the Beijing conference and made it a priority strategic orientation for its activities. In a 2002 document entitled *Integrating Gender Perspectives in the Work of WHO*, WHO defined its gender policy. This policy determined that the *gender perspective* must be integrated in all sectors, departments, offices, budgets, programs and policies of the organization; that these must produce action plans to this effect; that the executive must plan mechanisms to monitor its implementation. In other words, the *gender perspective* must become the *standard practice* of WHO. This reform policy, as former *Director General* Gro Harlem Brundtland explains in her introductory remarks, "will require the commitment, participation and contribution of every staff member"[35].

The *gender perspective* is also at the heart of WHO's relations with its member states. The UN health agency analyzes national gender policies with a view to pushing these countries to adjust their policies and align them with the Beijing norms. WHO develops *didactic tools* to this end. For example, the agency produced a manual of about 500 pages, destined to health directors, on *Transforming Health Systems: Gender and Rights in Reproductive Health*. As do many other organs of the UN, WHO organizes *pilot courses* at the national level on gender and sexual and reproductive rights.

From the power of experts to a global culture

Hidden in institutional labyrinths, working in underground networks, having privileged relations with officials of international organizations often during the entire period between the end of the 1960s and the 1990s, the *experts* have played a key role in formulating the new global norms and in the integration process which culminated in the new postmodern ethic. They have been at once catalysts, advisers, "facilitators", intellectual leaders, ethical leaders.

Nameless and faceless, exerting their influence indirectly, behind the scenes, upstream of decisions, without being subjected to democratic checks, a small number of experts have been the actual pilots of the global cultural revolution. The power these *enlightened despots* effectively exercised after the fall of the Berlin Wall, when the "new global norms" were set, has been of absurd proportions. Increasingly, the policy of international organizations and governments towards these experts has been to give them *direct access* to politicians and decision-makers so that they can exercise their influence unhindered.

The postmodern ideology of a few experts has become global culture through a double process: horizontal and vertical. The *vertical* transmission model consisted in "educating" decision-makers of national governments, businesses, universities, schools, development organizations. In their turn, these decision-makers communicated their knowledge of new norms to lower ranks, to "the people", also through education reform, rewriting textbooks and an active partnership with the media. The UN, as we have seen, gave the experts the means of forming its high officials and agency heads. In their turn, the UN organs advised the governments of member states.

The more efficient *horizontal* model belongs to the *political revolution* which set in motion the *cultural revolution*. It consists in passing via *peers* to transform mentalities and behaviors among one's equals: "peer education". On the ground, throughout the world, some pilot NGOs, for example, educate "civil society" and local communities.

The politico-cultural revolution took place and continues to spread silently through similar informal processes. In the West, the ideology of the postmodern intelligentsia found a favorable cultural ground. It penetrated without resistance into political mechanisms and into culture. In the rest of the world, states and societies too often accept, without daring to criticize it, the assistance of "experts" to implement the new norms and allow themselves to be formatted by them.

The Millennium Development Goals

The implementation of the new global ethic also characterizes itself by frequent reformulations of its objectives into *new strategies*, without ever departing from the *ideological framework* in which it was conceived. The objectives of the great conferences of the 1990s were thus reformulated, at the start of the 21st century, into the *Millennium Development Goals* (MDGs). The raison d'être of the MDGs, written into the ideological continuation of the large conferences, was to transform their platforms for action into "concrete and measurable" goals. Conceived as the means of making them more effective operationally, the MDGs contain and are indivisible from the conferences, particularly from Cairo and Beijing, as we shall show.

To mark the start of the new millennium, led by his desire to ensure the UN a central place in global governance, Kofi Annan organized an extraordinary summit of heads of state in New York in September 2000. At this summit 191 governments adopted the *Millennium Declaration*. A year later, the UN *Secretariat* produced eight *Millennium Development Goals* to be realized by 2015. Since then, governments, aid agencies and NGOs have reoriented their work according to the MDGs.

The MDGs have been, and still are, very widely publicized. They are:

> 1.- Eradicate extreme poverty and hunger;
> 2.- Achieve universal primary education;
> 3.- Promote gender equality and empower women;
> 4.- Reduce child mortality;
> 5.- Improve maternal health;
> 6.- Combat HIV/AIDS, malaria, and other diseases;
> 7.- Ensure environmental sustainability;
> 8.- Develop a global partnership for development.

Different organs of the UN use the MDGs to push governments to implement the Cairo and Beijing objectives. The UNDP, for example, uses several approaches. When the governments of developing countries prepare their national reports on the implementation of the MDGs, the UNDP recommends that they work with *gender* experts. The UNDP also encourages the drafting of supposedly "independent" studies in preparation for the drafting of these national reports, and the submission of national reports to groups of experts chosen by the UN for verification: the real goal is to verify that governments align themselves with the "experts'" ideology. The UNDP "trains" national drafting teams. In other words, the UN checks the implementation process of the MDGs at every stage, and governments are surreptitiously constrained to focus, not on their own priorities, but on those of the agents of the global cultural revolution.

Instead of focussing on the concrete and objective needs of poor populations, as one would hope, the MDGs and development cooperation continue to be hijacked and to give priority to ideological objectives. The 2005 UNFPA report, for example, entitled *The Promise of Equality: Gender Equity, Reproductive Health and the Millennium Development Goals*, hammers the message that "gender equality" and "reproductive health" are "indispensable" for the realization of the MDGs, that they are their "keystone"[36], that they represent the very foundations of global socioeconomic development without which the rest of the building would collapse, that without the *integral* implementation of the Cairo and Beijing programs of action, the MDGs cannot be attained, that reproductive health and gender deserve *absolute priority* in international, national and local development policies, investments and budgets - in other words that they should be put "at the forefront of poverty reduction efforts"[37].

The militants of the feminist revolution have succeeded in making of gender and all that the concept implicitly contains, including reproductive health (hence, remember, "safe" abortion), an end in itself: the third MDG. But the agents of social transformation primarily consider that gender is the path by which the realization of the other seven goals is to be achieved, in other words the absolute priority in development. Once again, they want gender to become a *cross-cutting issue*, which is to say central to all socioeconomic sectors. They want to prevent gender from being trapped in a "ghetto". Gender equality and reproductive health become the mandatory way for the fight against poverty, which is thereby instrumentalized in an attempt to turn into binding norms the implementation of objectives including the erotic revolution program.

As for the UNDP, it states that abortions in unsanitary conditions represents thirteen percent of maternal deaths. "Thus achieving Goal 5 will require rapidly expanding access to reproductive health care"[38] affirms the UN development program.

On the ground, it is the agents of the global sexual revolution who make the most propaganda for the MDGs. The 2005 UNFPA report enables us to identify their arguments. We can thereby premune ourselves against the seduction inherent in their propaganda:

- *Historical importance*: UNFPA amplifies the historical importance of the MDGs. They speak of "an unprecedented consensus to end poverty"[39]. UNFPA speaks of the MDGs as if they were a *new departure* while in reality they come at the end of a highly controversial process.

- *Quasi-juridical character*: UNFPA qualifies the MDGs as a "compact" concluded by the nations of the whole world. The use of this juridical terminology is deceptive, since the MDGs do not have a binding character. As is its habit and for strategic reasons, UNFPA tends to reinterpret international law in the light of the "consensus", contributing to the blurring of the boundary between international law and what is a consensus. Refering to "the promises for global action on poverty, equality and equity espoused at the UN conferences of the 1990s and the 2000 UN Millennium Summit", UNFPA affirms: "Under international law, these agreements are more than rhetoric: they are collective obligations."[40].

- *Voluntaristic idealism*: UNFPA turns the MDGs into a grand vision, a planetary humanistic project. The UN fund exalts the boldness of this "plan" to "halve extreme poverty by 2015". It speaks of the MDGs as of a "great promise" capable of liberating "hundreds of millions of people" from the "shackles of poverty", sparing the "lives of 30 million children and 2 million mothers", of pushing back the spread of AIDS and above all of making "millions of young people" participate in the development of their countries and in the creation of a "better world for them and future generations"[41]. The UN propaganda springs from a neo-collectivist and abstract utopia.

- *Hidden agenda and mental manipulation*: UNFPA uses presumed "self-evident" truths to gain acceptance by the greatest possible number of people for programs of action going in most cases against cultures and religions. One of these "self-evident truths" is that gender equality is essential to development. Who, after all, would be able to contest such an affirmation? But does not the dominant interpretation of "gender equality" hide a project to deconstruct female and male anthropological specificities, motherhood, what is given by nature and the law of God written in the nature of man?

- *A new ethic*: UNFPA insists that the realization of the MDGs is "mandatory". This obligation is held to be at once ethical and juridical: achieving human rights "is not a matter of charity: it is both a legal obligation and a collective responsibility"[42]. Also: "From a human rights standpoint, addressing poverty is more than a moral obligation"[43]: the MDGs become a juridical obligation through the rights approach. The new global ethic would put law above morals and above charity. The value of the new ethic is supposed to be higher than that of the old ethic because it would have the capacity to make its norms binding: "The rights-based approach marks a shift away from an earlier development focus on meeting basic needs, which relied on charity or good will."[44]. The new ethic rests on individuals "as 'rights-holders', which implies that others are 'duty-bearers'"[45].

Adoption of an acceleration strategy

Since the Cairo and Beijing conferences, the agents of the global cultural revolution have kept governments under constant pressure to implement the platforms for action of these conferences as quickly as possible. They have never let up complaining about how slow "progress" has been, about "unkept promises", about the lack of resources and political will. On all occasions they wave the red flag of "target dates", arguing that the international community will never manage to respect its "commitments" if it continues at the present pace. Since the adoption of the MDGs, the agents of social transformation have introduced the word *acceleration* into the language of international cooperation.

Before "the scale of the challenge of transforming gender relations"[46], reads the 2005 UNFPA report, the UN fund seeks with unflagging zeal to communicate everywhere the "impetus for change"[47], encouraging interested parties to engage "in strong efforts to alter the status quo"[48]: "Continuing the 'business as usual' approach to gender equality can derail efforts to reach the MDGs"[49]. The language employed leaves no room for doubt about UNFPA's determination: "The dedicated efforts of civil society, parlimentarians and the media in holding governments and other key actors accountable are crucial to maintaining momentum"[50]. UNFPA wants to keep reproductive health and gender equality "priority issues high on national agendas, and hold governments and other key actors accountable to commitments made"[51].

For its part, the *World Health Assembly* (an organ gathering all the member states of WHO) on 22 May 2004 adopted an *acceleration strategy*[52] aiming to reach the targets fixed by the international community at the Cairo and Beijing conferences and by the MDGs. For WHO, MDG three, five and six directly connect to sexual and reproductive health. The new strategy, although adopted by an *intergovernmental* organ, was in reality clearly created by WHO *experts*: another example, if needed, of global governance by enlightened despots.

WHO wants to obtain from states a *maximal commitment*. Sexual and reproductive health is, according to the UN health agency, a priority of communities' and nations' socioeconomic development and should benefit from powerful financial resources and a strong political mobilization on the part of all states. Worried about the "slowness of progress", WHO pushes states to put reproductive health at the center of their budgets and of national planning. The health agency advocates the *reinforcement of health systems*, with the help of NGOs, so that access to reproductive health can be made universal. WHO commits itself to support countries in this effort. WHO insistently asks states to monitor the implementation of this strategy, especially where dealing with adolescents. The new WHO strategy provides states with a *roadmap*: they must start by identifying the "problems" which impede the implementation of the Cairo objectives, establish priorities, formulate strategies for an accelerated action through consultative processes implying all the "stakeholders" of sexual and reproductive health. In practice, the new strategy means that states will be put under more and more pressure to collaborate with NGOs.

The strategy of the agents of the global sexual revolution has not been merely rhetoric: it succeeded in transforming mentalities, policies, development priorities, language, behaviors on the ground, especially among the young, in the West as well as in developing countries. In a majority of countries, school programs, governmental policies and penal codes were reformed, new laws were promulgated, the budgets of ministries and governments, national as well as local, have given priority to gender and reproductive health programs, employers have become agents of change by spreading information on reproductive health among their colleagues, women have engaged in politics and transformed the processes by which governments establish their priorities, gender was integrated into constitutions and at all levels of society.

Diagnosis of the present situation

While the agents of the globalization of the western sexual revolution exert maximal pressure on governments and cultures, it has become evident that their doctrinaire impetus is today out of steam. At the end of their course, they are producing no new concepts. Their discourse is becoming repetitive. On the operational level, no matter what they say, they have already achieved most of their objectives. Their "impetus", to use their own expression, is now directed towards horizontal implementation on the ground of concepts going back to the 1960s. The generation in power at the end of the cold war no longer exerts its influence.

The pressing issue today is the preservation of human, cultural and religious traditions in developing countries.

Through the proliferation of operational partnerships in all directions[53], the Cairo and Beijing objectives and their underpinning anthropology have already penetrated deeply into the fabric of societies, bringing about the emergence of a new ethic founded, at the individual level, on "nirvana well-being", self-redemption, possession of one's own "fulfilment", the full realization of one's "individual potential", the "freedom to choose" and virtual access to all choices for "self-realization" and, at the social level, on the sole criterion of economic productivity.

But while the new ethic seems to have won the day, the doctrinaire exhaustion of the revolutionary agents indicates paradoxically the setting in motion of a *deradicalization process* and the emergence of a civilization other than that imagined by the militants of the revolution. Indeed, the deconstruction of reality and truth was doomed to deconstruct itself.

KEY-WORDS OF THIS CHAPTER

Globalization of the revolution; operational networks of normative global governance; agitprop; critical mass; integration process; demographic transition; coup d'etat; comparative advantage; mandate; decentralization; localization; cross-cutting issue; acceleration strategy; relentless efforts; maximal commitment; doctrinaire impetus; deradicalization process.

---

[1] The key ideas of some of these individuals have been briefly analyzed in chapter one.

[2] In the 1970s, the *Club of Rome* organized much influential noise on this subject.

[3] Cf. recommendations 5.2 of *Agenda 21*.

[4] In April 1968, thirty personalities met in Rome to talk about the long-term future of the planet. The *Club of Rome* was formed on the basis of this meeting. *The Limits to Growth* studied five factors affecting the future of the world: food production, population, industrialization, pollution and natural resources.

[5] 75 million per year around 1975, 87 million in 1985 and about 81 million around 1995. In spite of the forecast decline in the rate of demographic growth, the annual increase in global population will stay at the current level of about 80 million until 2025. See Jyoti Shankar Singh. *Creating a New Consensus on Population*. Earthscan Publications. London. 1998, pp. 84-85.

[6] Ib.

[7] Implications of Worldwide Population Growth for US Security and Overseas Interests.

[8] NSSM 200, p. 115.

[9] See Robert Whelan. Whose Choice: Population Controllers' or yours ? Committee on Population and the Economy. London 1992, pp. 7-9.

[10] The IUSSP was founded at a meeting organized by Margaret Sanger in Paris, in 1928, one year after the first *World population Conference* of Geneva (29 august - 3 September 1927). The organization set itself the mandate of studying "population problems" in a "purely scientific" manner. The Nazis tried to take control of the organization, which had eugenic tendencies. After the war, in 1947, there was a constitutional reform. The Union became an association of individual members. Since the reform, the association has extended its activities in developing countries. Its "purely scientific" character is a myth: the ideological objectives of the association are evident (demographic control and sexual revolution). The IUSSP today has some 1900 members from 130 countries.

[11] It is due to the lobby of two influential personalities in the American administration of the time, William Draper and Philander Claxton, militants for demographic control, that America gave its support to the idea of a first conference on population in Bucharest. We note once again the influence of a few key people, who manage to orient an international process in the direction of their ideology, and the absence of real democratic debate.

[12] See Singh, p. 9.

[13] 1,350 NGO representatives took part in the *Population Tribune*, held from 18 to 30 August 1974 and organized on the model of the parallel activity of NGOs at the 1972 Stockholm environment conference.

[14] See Singh, pp. 121-138.

[15] Ib., p. 86.

[16] See recommendation 84 of the Mexico document.

[17] Nafis Sadik was *Executive director* of UNFPA from 1987 to 2000 and *Secretary General* of the Cairo Conference on Population in 1994.

[18] Participants at the New Delhi meeting included: Halfdan Mahler, *Secretary General* of the IPPF (after having been *Director General* of WHO from 1973 to 1988); Fred Sai, *President* of the IPPF, who was *President* of the *Main Committee* of the Cairo conference; Nafis Sadik, *Executive Director* of the UNFPA, who was *Secretary General* of the Cairo conference; and Steven Sinding, then *Population Director* at the *Rockefeller Foundation*, and *Director General* of IPPF until 2006.

[19] IPPF. Vision 2000. Strategic Plan. Approved by the IPPF members' assembly in October 1992, p. 3.

[20] According to the IPPF, the demand for family planning had to increase from 300 million users in 1992 to more than 550 million in 2000.

[21] The IPPF believed that thirty to fifty percent of the 500,000 annual maternal deaths were due to abortion in bad sanitary conditions.

[22] The IPPF believed that one of the main barriers to improving the sexual and reproductive health of women was their lack of power to make socioeconomic decisions.

[23] See IPPF, Vision 2000. Ib., p. 4.

[24] See Singh, pp. 39-40.

[25] The American delegation, constituted by *President* Bill Clinton and led by the *Under Secretary of State for Global Affairs* Tim Wirth, worked closely with the IPPF and the UNFPA during the whole process of the Cairo conference. Shortly after his election at the end of 1992, Clinton reversed Ronald Reagan's "Mexico City Policy" which banned American finance for population activities including abortion. The coalition made up of Al Gore, Nafis Sadik and Tim Wirth assured success at Cairo to the globalization of the sexual and feminist revolution.

[26] Singh. Ib., p. 161.

[27] See paragraph 15.8 of the final Cairo document.

[28] Ib., paragraphs 15.2 and 15.4.

[29] *Catholics for a Free Choice* is an NGO active among international organizations which promotes the right to abortion. The organization bears the name "Catholic" to the subversive end of attempting to present, within the Catholic Church, an alternative view to that of the Magisterium on matters of sexual morality and abortion. *Catholics for a Free Choice* is not recognized as Catholic by the Church.

[30] The word *gender* appeared 218 times in the Beijing document, while the word *mother* appeared only 17 times, and at that not in the context of "normal" motherhood, but in difficult contexts: "underage mothers", "teenage mothers", or in the case of breastfeeding.

[31] The Rome Food Summit of December 1996 closed the conference process and introduced the international community into the *implementation phase*.

[32] The UNFPA is a fund. It finances, principally for developing countries, sexual and reproductive health programs within the framework of sustainable development. These programs include for example AIDS prevention, "youth support", *gender equality*, sex education, reproductive health services.

[33] UNIFEM, the *United Nations Development Fund for Women*, is more specifically in charge of promoting the *gender perspective*. UNIFEM has developed vigorously in the last few years. This fund produces a biannual report on *Progress of the World's Women*. UNIFEM works to make the *gender perspective* inform the intergovernmental process. The Beijing document asked UNIFEM to incorporate a female dimension in development at all levels and to develop a multilateral dialogue on the empowerment of women.

[34] In January 2004, for example, a seminar was held in Paris to "build the capacity" of national UNESCO offices in the area of gender. This seminar educated UNESCO personnel in a greater understanding of *gender*, taught them how to carry out a *gender* analysis, and how to develop a rights approach which responds to the *gender perspective*.

[35] Integrating Gender Perspectives in the Work of WHO. 2002. WHO.

[36] UNFPA. State of World Population 2005. *The Promise of Equality: Gender Equity, Reproductive Health and the Millennium Development Goals*, p. 33.

[37] Ib., p. 9.

[38] UNDP. Human Development Report. 2003, p. 99.

[39] Ib., p. 7.

[40] Ib., p. 92.

[41] For the quotations of this paragraph, see: UNFPA. State of World Population 2005. Press release.

[42] UNFPA. State of World Population 2005, p. 3.

[43] Ib., p. 22.

[44] Ib.

[45] Ib.

[46] Ib., p. 5.

[47] Ib., p. 17.

[48] Ib., p. 19.

[49] Ib., p. 17.

[50] Ib., p. 21.

[51] Ib., p. 2.

[52] "Reproductive Health: draft strategy to accelerate progress towards the attainment of international development goals and targets." 15 April 2004. A57/13.

[53] The partnerships have effectively become countless and of a diversity difficult to grasp: women, men, young people, couples, even families, ministers, local authorities, schools, development NGOs, sports, cinema and musical celebrities, social structures at all levels...

TECHNIQUES AND STRATEGIES OF THE AGENTS OF SOCIAL TRANSFORMATION

This chapter provides an analytical overview of the techniques which the agents of revolutionary change have used with incontrovertible success to transform mentalities in the West, and of the strategies they have used since the fall of the Berlin wall to impose their language, norms and values on the rest of the world. Revolution was achieved by culture, not by force.

To grasp the real stakes of the times we live in, it is necessary to free ourselves from old mind-sets, according to which only formal, institutional or juridical developments have a real impact on social life. The deconstruction of traditional, democratic and family institutions, itself the result of the western cultural revolution, has in effect allowed *cultural and informal processes*, often *manipulative*, to gain *effective power* in the postmodern civilization at the start of the 21st century.

This chapter underlines the effectiveness of the social transformation techniques and attempts to identify what makes them manipulative. Recall that the *ambivalence* of postmodern culture, studied in chapter two, is itself a technique of manipulation. *Larvatus prodeo*, René Descartes used to say: "I go forward wearing a mask". Manipulation sharply poses the question of *personal conscience*, its violation and its *freedom*.

The majority are not sufficiently aware of the sociopolitical power conferred on those who master the techniques of social engineering. In fact, as we have seen in the earlier chapters, agitating minorities have been the engine of the revolution, and the concepts which became globally normative in the 1990s come from the agenda that these minorities have constructed since the 1960s. How did these minorities manage to successfully change the values of a *critical mass* of individuals and communities, and end up making the unconscious majority swing in their favor? The driving ideas of the sexual revolution, the direction taken for decades by educational reform, legislation on "parity", abortion, homosexual "marriage", homosexual parenting, euthanasia, among others, serve minority interests, not the will and the aspirations of the majority.

Finally in this chapter we will emphasize the multiplicity of initiatives, the creativity, the voluntarism and the astonishing perseverance and zeal with which the agents of social transformation have worked to conquer the cultural field.

A "gentle" and quiet revolution

The revolution was a *cultural* revolution. It was a *quiet* revolution. It took place without bloodshed, without coups, without structural or institutional upheavals, without political repression, without violence, without open confrontation, without infringing on democratic principles. There was never even, in any country of the world, any open and sustained democratic debate on the content or implications of its propositions. The revolution did not put in place a totalitarian political regime. It did not create a "world government". Although it did fundamentally reinterpret the mandates of institutions, it did not formally change them. While it exerted a decisive influence on the reinterpretation of law, it created relatively few new juridical instruments. In other words, the institutional façade has remained standing, but the rooms now have new occupants. The changes of values, mentalities, lifestyles, and behaviors took place *within* institutions, businesses, cultures, families and religions. Without wanting to minimize the responsibility of those who have not taken the revolution seriously, its *almost invisible* character contributes to explaining why no organized opposition or resistance has ever been expressed.

The revolution was achieved by stealth, in ways which were informal, diffuse, parallel, "horizontal", internal or *from within*[1], noiseless, practically without people knowing it. Everything took place *by way of consensus*, through an *evolutionary process of change*. The agents of change used techniques or strategies such as *facilitation, sensitization, awareness-raising, grassroots participation, mobilization, peer education, informal education, values clarification, cultural adjustment, transforming and "holistic" integration, capacity-building, consensus-building, cultural harmonization*, the creation and globalization of a *new language*, *dialogue, mainstreaming, slogans, "retreats"* and *training seminars, cul-turally sensitive approaches, negotiation,* the *management* of relations, the acquisition of *know-how* and *life skills,* the creation of *enabling environments, methodological tools, ownership, internalization, partner-ships, participatory democracy, good governance, "civil society",* the *grass roots* movement, *transnational networks, cooperation* and other *"soft"* and subtle methods. There is space in this chapter to study but a few of these.

These social transformation techniques have been manipulative to the extent that they have been used to *hide* and *impose* on *all* an agenda belonging only to *a few.*

Note that if the methods used by the agents of cultural change did not infringe on democratic processes, they did tend to *substitute* them. Consensus-building tends to supersede majority vote or hierarchical decision-making processes; informal education tends to take the place of the classical curriculum; global governance quietly overtakes tra-ditional intergovernmental multilateralism. The transition to a new civilization is already well underway, and going backwards now seems impossible.

Social engineering: an "art" and a "science"

The development of human and social sciences, particularly psychol-ogy and sociology, has put at the disposal of the agents of change tools for transforming the mentalities of the masses which mankind did not have access to in the past. Social engineering has become a real science, turning *propaganda, manipulation* and even *brainwashing* into techniques of social transformation.

By social engineering we understand the *art* and *science* of leading in-dividuals, groups, or even entire societies, cultures or a civilization, to-ward the accomplishment of a particular agenda, without these groups becoming aware at any stage of the trip that an agenda from without is being imposed on them.

The "art" of social engineering consists in making the concerned par-ties *participate* so that they genuinely believe that they are themselves at the origin of the agenda which is in fact being imposed upon them, so that the people believe they are in control of the agenda's presup-positions and adhere to them sincerely and in full confidence. The 145 social engineers present their agenda in such a way that the concerned parties are convinced that it is to their own advantage to adhere to it and commit to its realization, and that they would be social and economic losers if they did not do so. Social engineers systematically avoid confrontation. Their behavior is "friendly": they seek to gain the confidence of those whose values they want to transform. Their approach is based on cooperation, consensus, participation, dialogue and governance. It belongs to their strategy not to give orders so as to avoid appearing as "masters". They present themselves as low-profile *sensitizers* or *facilitators*. Their arguments, prepared by a highly sophisticated intelligentsia, are punchy, rational, well constructed; they seem "scientific" and unquestionable. In the course of the social engineering process, the experts allegedly "clarify" the values of cultures and traditions. The actual goal is to circumvent the cultural obstacles on the way to the implementation of their own agenda.

Manipulation as a process is a vicious circle. The erotic revolution has made the majority easy to manipulate. This situation, in turn, facilitates the forward movement of the deconstruction process. A hedonistic and narcissistic generation has arisen. As individuals progressively lose their identity and sense of direction, the task of the social engineers becomes increasingly easy. The majority have placed themselves into a state of dependence on experts. *Conformism*, also called *consensus*, has imperceptibly replaced democratic debate. In such a consensus culture, it would even seem that *leadership* has become impossible. The success of the global cultural revolution is primarily due to the fact that the majority in the West, morally weakened by apostasy, has let itself be manipulated: such has been the spiral of deconstruction.

Consensus culture

The shift from modernity to postmodernity has been marked by the abandonment of decision-making methods deemed aggressive, exclusive, unilateral, authoritarian, paternalistic or imposed "top-down", in favor of methods deemed more participatory, more equitable, more democratic and more sustainable. We have thus shifted from the "decide – announce – defend" model and from the majority vote to *consensus-building* and other informal and "bottom-up" processes. Modern methods of decision-making have become globally counter-cultural. By contrast, consensus has become culture: we live in a culture which values bottom-up participation and equality more than authority and hierarchies, agreement more than confrontation. The old methods, such as majority vote, have not vanished, but they are often governed from within by a consensus process which surreptitiously deconstructs their identity. Have not most of our heads of state and political leaders, of both "left" and "right", while keeping a certain tone fitting to their political allegiances, in practice aligned themselves with the "consensus"? Is there any place where we can still find original thought which is not dependent on the experts of global governance?

Consensus-building is a complex process, which goes through several stages: among others, grassroots consultation, bottom-up participation in formulating the content of the consensus, the inclusion of all "stakeholders", the progressive elimination of opposition, and negotiations to reach a global agreement – the ultimate goal of the process. The consensus culture emphasizes participation, dialogue, friendship, disinterestedness[2], mutual respect, inclusion of the weakest, the equality of all participants, and solidarity: it is "people-centered". However, to be genuine, the consensus process has to be inspired by and to reflect, from start to finish, a search for the truth and the good of all people and has to be founded on what is capable of uniting them in a truly universal way.

If the consensus process takes as its point of departure the denial that truth exists, it becomes the opposite of what it professes: a form of imposition, today reaching historically unprecedented, global proportions. Consensus-building then becomes a social engineering technique. The majority, not really consulted, does not participate truly. It is manipulated, "formatted" by proactive minorities, who are the only real participants. The consensus is then artificial and pre-established. At each stage of the process, the agents of social transformation orient consensus-building in the direction of their own interests. Their special interests agenda ends up replacing the common values. At the end of the day, the alleged consensus becomes an absolute and the keystone of a new culture.

Consensus-building

The consensus-building process has been one of the main instruments of global cultural transformation since the end of the cold war. It bears repeating: it is through the construction of the "new global consensus" which took place at the great UN conferences of the 1990s that the western cultural revolution of the 1960s turned into a global cultural revolution.

Let us identify the stages of the consensus-building process and analyze how the social engineers hijacked them. We shall observe that the visionary minorities pilot the consensus-building process from beginning to end.

1.- *Agenda-setting*. Agenda-setting is the starting point of the consensus-building process: on which vision and on which program of action shall we work toward an agreement? The task of writing the "draft" or the broad outline of this agenda is generally entrusted to a handful of visionary "experts" *before* the consultation process begins. In practice, the experts proceed outside any democratic control, primarily according their ideological priorities. The new vision must propose a *change* and *progress* for mankind as a whole in order to galvanize the consensus-building process: it must be revolutionary. At the same time, it must set out from the common aspirations of mankind, such as the desire to protect the environment, social equity or maternal health.

We have repeatedly seen in the previous chapters that the experts who exerted their influence on global governance in the consensus-building process of the 1990s belonged to the postmodern intelligentsia working since the late 1960s at building a supposedly "progressive" vision. These experts have often pursued radical objectives (zero growth, a secularist or neo-pagan ethic, utopian pacifism, sexual license, the right to abortion, the deconstruction of the West), which they hid behind the new language they themselves created without defining it clearly: *sustainable development, reproductive health, global ethic, human security, cultural liberty* and so on.

Throughout the consensus-building process, the visionary experts carefully ensured that the *integrity* of their agenda was preserved, so that it would not be diverted nor diluted but on the contrary keep on being strengthened, to the point of becoming the explicit priority objective of the consensus in question. Their (utopian) goal was that at the end of the process all should adopt, identify with and apply their own objectives. Since the consensus is pre-established, such a process is twisted. Further, radicalism is never authentically consensual.

2.- *Awareness-raising*. *Lobbyists* belonging to the same ideological networks as the "experts" raise the awareness of the public at large in favor of the new vision and its language. *Awareness-raising campaigns* use all available means (the media, Internet, pamphlets, advertising, cinema, training sessions, lectures…). Powerfully financed, these campaigns are generally effective. They start off simultaneously from real problems (such as the abuse of children's rights, the prevalence of AIDS or environmental degradation) and from aspirations common to all mankind (global ethic, equity, peace, freedom, participation and so on). They are, however, manipulative to the extent that they use real problems to impose an ideological agenda on the greatest possible number of people.

Awareness-raising campaigns increase the number of adherents to the new vision. They include calls to *mobilization*. Many rally to what appears to represent the movement of the strongest and the way of social progress. Awareness-raisers use an alarmist tone. Their approach is emotional, propagandist and often irrational, and therefore doomed to fail in the long run.

3.- *Consultation.* Once the vision has been established and once the awareness-raising process resulted in the constitution of a critical mass of adherents, "grassroots" consultation begins. Such consultation appears to confer a democratic character on the consensus-building process and to legitimize it. The *informal* character of these consultations, however, allows their leaders to frame them ideologically. The stakeholders' contributions are taken into account and integrated into the consensus-building process to the extent that they do not challenge the experts' agenda but reinforce it. Historically, the groups that have been consulted already belonged, more or less closely, to the visionaries' ideological "networks". Never was opposition included: it was systematically excluded.

4.- *Negotiations.* The process then moves on to the negotiation phase. When a common search for the truth is lacking, the negotiation process translates into a series of compromises and a progressive loss of identity among the participants, who end up aligning themselves with the ideas put forth by the visionaries and the minorities. During the negotiations process, *facilitators* ceaselessly pressure for a search for the *common denominator*. To do so, they use the "conflict resolution" techniques developed by the humanities and social sciences. The facilitators' role is never "neutral". A facilitator is in fact a *leader in disguise* – what some have called a *horizontal leader*. His real role is to guide the participants in the consensus-building process toward adopting the vision established from the start by the minorities in power.

Contrasting with a democratic debate, where there is a majority and an opposition, a winner and a loser, the consensus process is oriented to the progressive elimination of opposition until the agreement of everybody is obtained. The social engineers pretend that the consensus process is *win-win* for everybody involved. In reality the participants have been manipulated, often even without realizing it, so that they end up compromising their values and identity.

5.- *Adoption of the consensus.* A consensus-building process never fails: it always reaches its goal, even if the participants generally end up losing in the process. Not joining the consensus means remaining *outside* what is uniting *all the others*, in a situation of unbearable isolation. In practice, this option is never chosen. Historically, no member state has remained outside the consensus adopted at the international UN conferences of the 1990s. It is true that, at the beginning of the conferences process, some expressed *reservations*, but these were not taken into account in the implementation. Besides, the use of reservations has been slowly abandoned. It goes against the logic of the consensus process, which has a constraining character.

6.- *Commitment* and *implementation.* Once the consensus has been adopted, the pressure groups repeat relentlessly to the participants that they must shift from agenda to action, that they are morally bound by the "commitments" they alleged made when joining the consensus. Imperceptibly, the "consensus" thereby becomes a *Diktat.* Awareness-raising campaigns are from then on supported by the existence of a "global consensus" which *all* are meant to honor. These campaigns increase the number of adherents to the new vision. The vise is tightened. It becomes increasingly difficult, culturally, to dispute the "gains" of the revolution.

The implementation of the consensus requires informed and efficient *managers*, who are in charge of applying the new norms in a conformist spirit, without challenging them or asking questions. The experts often consider governments and other managers to be slow, to lack political will or to never do enough; they offer them their help in the implementation of the "consensus".

7.- *Ownership* and *internalization.* By dint of indoctrination, participants in the consensus-building process become *good students* of the enlightened despots. They end up *appropriating* the visionaries' agenda by bringing it into their own value system, by *internalizing* it.

8.- *Monitoring, grassroots mobilization* and *decentralization*. The pressure groups turn into *watchdogs*. They monitor governments with a view to making them transform the global consensus into *national reality*. They ask governments to provide the UN with evidence of implementation of the global consensus in their national reports to the *General Assembly*, to the different commissions of the *Economic and Social Council* (ECOSOC) and to the treaty monitoring bodies. They create and multiply *indicators of progress*[3], "best practices" and statistics for measuring the "progress" made by participants. They demand *transparency* on the part of businesses and governments and require them to show proof of their *responsibility*. The pressure is constantly increased. The watchdogs talk of the need for a *dramatic acceleration* to reach the targets established by the international community.

The revolutionary agitators often try to mobilize the grassroots directly and to provoke local debate on the "performance" of their governments. They push the people to rise up and claim their rights, to hold their government accountable. They want to organize participatory democracy *at the local level* and believe it necessary to open local political culture to groups susceptible of rallying to the global ideological objectives, such as local feminist groups.

9.- *Partnerships. Networkers* multiply *partnerships* in all directions to accelerate the horizontal implementation of the consensus through all sectors of society. An ever increasing mass of influential actors implement the consensus.

10.- *Rewards, best practices*. Good students of the enlightened despots, those who have performed best in implementing the consensus, are rewarded with "prizes" or the honorary title of *best practices*. They become an example for all global governance actors. Best practices become globally normative, thereby filling the vacuum left by the collapse of "universal values".

Gender training

Having become culture, the consensus process henceforth expresses itself in a great variety of contexts. Let us examine how it applies to *women's empowerment* and to *gender training* which, since the Cairo and Beijing conferences, have been the global cultural revolution's center of gravity.

Gender training is a process deconstructing female and male "stereotypes". When stereotypes refer to cultural values and practices that are contrary to human dignity and to the dignity of the woman in particular, "deconstructing" them performs a useful service. *De facto*, however, *gender training* is most often at the service of postmodern ideology: motherhood, fatherhood, male and female identity, the spousal relationship between a married man and woman, the male/female anthropological complementarity are treated as the basic stereotypes to deconstruct.

1.- *Awareness-raising. Awareness-raising* consists in making women conscious of "inequalities" which the agents of social transformation consider them to be victimized by, of the "power" which they do not yet enjoy, and of their "rights" – particularly sexual and reproductive rights. Awareness-raising "awakens" women to a new reality – the multiplicity of choices which would be available to them: multiple social roles, economic possibilities, sexual practices and orientations. Such an "awakening" allegedly "liberates" women from their "ignorance" and from social, cultural and religious pre-determinations which would set limits on their ability to "choose". "Enlightened" by the experts, women gain self-confidence.

A major challenge of postmodern civilization, *awareness-raising* tends to replace traditional education which for its part develops the whole person – her autonomy, her capacity for individual judgment, as well as her reason, conscience and heart.

2.- *Ownership and transformation of mentalities.* Once awakened to the *knowledge* of their "choices", women taking part in *gender training* must cooperate, in a dynamic and interactive way, in the transformation of their own ways of thinking. They are expected to *commit* themselves. *Gender training* aims to *change* the image they have of men's and women's roles in society, and to make them abandon their certitudes so that they can be open to the platform of the revolution. The social engineers teach them to identify their alleged *needs* and to express them in both the private and public domains. The purpose is in reality to make them espouse the experts' vision of women's needs.

As they let themselves be seduced by the social engineers' arguments, women abandon their traditions and the religious values which are an obstacle to the adoption of the program of the cultural revolution. They appropriate the new global norms, become their *owners* and internalize them.

Gender training insists that the liberated woman should be proud of her choices, sure of herself, confident in her determinations. She should "own" her choices, esteem them and esteem herself: only then will she at last be "in control" of her life. Notice however how *gender training* in fact places women in a condition of dependence with respect to the "experts": it obliges women, as it were, to choose the ideological program of the agents of social transformation.

3.- *Behaviour change. Gender training* then pressures women to actively claim their "rights" (rights to property, to an equal salary, sexual and reproductive rights...) and to get involved in action which favors social change: women must modify their attitudes and behaviours, "renegotiate their role" at home and in society. A new global code of conduct emerges and is imposed.

4.- *Militancy.* Co-opted by the revolutionary movement, women lose their freedom and autonomy. They hold governments and other social institutions accountable and demand proof that they are honoring the pseudo-commitments they made at Cairo and Beijing. They demand access to competencies, information, health care, resources, decision-making processes, thereby realizing the objective of the revolutionary process, which is to transform the structures and institutions which supposedly reinforce and perpetuate "discrimination" and "inequality".

5.- *Social transformation.* The feminist revolution does not restrict its effects to women, but spreads them to society as a whole. Men too are supposed to be sensitized to the values of the revolution, to internalize them, to take an active part, to collaborate, to change their attitude and behaviour vis-à-vis women, to become their partners in their quest for equality and sexual and reproductive rights. As for parents, they must change the image they have of their daughter's or son's social roles. The social engineers say that the future of the world depends on a generalized *cultural adjustment* in favor of a new relationship between the sexes.

Gender training is an integral part of a "training" offered from the earliest infancy: it begins at home, at birth. It is then integrated transversally in the school curriculum. The agents of change believe that children entering nursery school have already acquired an image of the role which they are called to play in society as girl or boy. They "verify" the extent to which this image is, or is not, opposed to their "free choice" ethic.

School becomes the place where the social engineers methodically deconstruct what they call *gender stereotypes*. The new ethic demands of teachers that they encourage girls to feel at ease in roles traditionally assigned to boys, and vice versa. They are no longer authorized to expect from one or other sex a particular type of behaviour. They are requested to teach girls not to be submissive, and boys not to be domineering. They are forbidden to present certain subjects as typically masculine (such as maths and sciences) and others as typically feminine (sewing, literature, languages). They are invited, for example, to ask boys to write about fashion, to sew, to carry out household tasks, and girls to play at doctors. Teachers are supposed to behave in a radically "neutral" way toward girls and boys – to be *gender neutral*. This neutrality is patently fictitious: it is a way of deconstructing masculine and feminine anthropological specificities. The message which *gender training* seeks to convey is that boys and girls, men and women, may choose freely their role in society and change role as often as they like.

Gender training manuals have proliferated since the Beijing conference. They target a wide variety of categories of individuals[4]. They generally contain "verification" tools encouraging citizens to analyze their country's legislation and policies in the light of the goals set by the Cairo and Beijing conferences. UNESCO, the UN agency specializing in education and culture, has taken leadership of *gender training* within the UN, organizing workshops and seminars to train teachers, parents, educators, children, bureaucrats, local authorities – world citizens, in the values of the new *gender* culture. UNESCO has placed the *gender perspective* at the heart of global educational reform.

Gender mainstreaming

Mainstreaming is the strategy used to implement the new paradigms universally and to turn them into priorities of global governance. Mainstreaming means the systematic integration of a "transversal" norm or value into all sectors of society and at all levels of decision-making. It is the strategy adopted at Beijing to advance the globalization of the philosophical underpinnings behind *gender* as analyzed in chapter three. It is far, however, from being restricted only to *gender*.

The *gender mainstreaming* strategy aims to ensure that henceforth no development program, no statistical system, no policy, no institution (social, political, economic, cultural or even religious), no legislation can escape the "obligation" of integrating the *gender perspective*.

Gender mainstreaming concentrates on the *system* (educational, health, political, economic, legislative, cultural, social and religious *structures*, norms and practices) which determines and institutionalizes female and male roles in a given society. It transforms existing social and institutional structures (most of which, according to the feminist movement, promote inequality) into structures favoring *gender* equality.

"Equality" must be understood according to the criteria of the new ideology: it includes control and ownership of one's body and one's rights, and deconstruction of man-woman anthropological complementarity. The agents of social change justify the absolute priority which they strive to give to *gender* equality within socioeconomic development programs by arguing that the whole world has finally, after thirty years of feminist militancy, become conscious of the "fact" that social development necessarily goes through equality as they interpret it.

The perspective is not only *systemic*, but also neo-collectivist. The *gender mainstreaming* strategy in actual fact does not take into account the individual woman as wife and mother – the person of the woman. It is interested in women only as a generic group in society, as a social category systematically presented as "vulnerable", "disadvantaged", "minority", or discriminated against.

Gender is considered as a *more fundamental* sociocultural variable than others such as age, race, class, ethnicity, cultural identity. *Gender* has also become an *intersectorial issue* of international cooperation, which means that it belongs to all sectors, and must obligatorily be integrated into the sectors where it is still absent.

The feminists want the perceptions, experiences, knowledge, rights and interests of women to influence policy formulation *from upstream*, in other words before the decisions are taken. Otherwise, the structural and systemic changes pursued by *gender mainstreaming* would not ensue with the desired breadth. Upstream work places *gender* at the very center of political decisions, medium-term plans, budgets, institutional structural reform, development policies, research, lobbying, legislation, planning – in short, of all social processes.

The social engineers have described the preparatory stages of the *gender mainstreaming* process. All three of these require the intervention of *experts*, who thus govern the process of social transformation.

1.- *Diagnostic.* The first stage consists in diagnosing the situation which the agent of social transformation meets in a particular country: the agent locates what he or she identifies as inequalities[5] and situations which must change. According to the *gender mainstreaming* perspective, no situation, no problem is neutral from the *gender* standpoint: the agent of change must examine *everything* to determine to what degree a given situation already conforms or not to the new ethic: *gender mainstreaming* is an all-encompassing strategy. In the majority of countries, UN organs participate in constituting *National Statistical Systems* and in training statisticians, taking particular care to integrate *gender* among development *indicators*.

2.- *Entry points.* Once the situation of a country has been examined, the agent of social transformation identifies the concrete possibilities for operating *gender mainstreaming* in the concrete situation of that country – the entry points for *gender* ideology in the given context.

3.- *Methodology.* The agent then develops a methodology adapted to the concrete situation of the country or the context in which *gender mainstreaming* is to be implemented, namely the integration of the *gender perspective* into all aspects of the country's socioeconomic life.

As distinct from certain revolutions of the past, which demanded brutal and immediate changes, *gender mainstreaming* is a patient, tenacious and perseverant revolutionary process, which builds on incremental gains. The feminist revolution must in practice take into account the success of "awareness-raising" campaigns and the pace at which mentalities change in order to impose itself on political and institutional structures. Becoming aware of the supposed "necessity" of changing political goals, development strategies, organizations and structures, cultures and traditions in favor of the new ideology can only move forward gradually.

Consultation process

Training manuals designed for sexual and reproductive health advisers plainly recognize that the goal of the consultative process is to *change* the values, mentalities, behaviors and lifestyles of the clients – not to advise them in such a way as to genuinely respect their beliefs and traditions. The manuals also explain that the change should be at once *internal* to the person (who, as a result of the advice he receives, adopts a different view of his sexual behavior or of the situation in which he finds himself), and *external* to the person (the great movement of global cultural transformation).

What the manuals do not readily admit is the real objective of the consultation process: the replacement of traditional family values with feelings of "power" provided by the autonomous exercise of individual freedom, according to the Freudian libido principle. Hence the consultation techniques advocated in the manuals instrumentalize to perverse ends the relationship of trust which is progressively set up between the adviser and his client. They establish a "confidentiality" framework which is unhealthy, as the consultative process actually isolates the individual from his family, community or religious relations.

The manuals describe the attitudes and competencies which advisers must have in order to be "efficient". They teach advisers to treat people as persons and not as clients, to have a friendly attitude, to avoid moralizing, judging, criticizing or imposing. They insist on the importance of the adviser's attitude, which must be warm and come across not only in words but also in body language (controlling their facial expressions, nodding, sitting comfortably, knowing how to interpret silences, phrases to use or to avoid using, knowing how to ask open questions and so on). The adviser should learn to listen. He should make himself approachable and know how to show compassion and empathy (which goes further than simple "sympathy"), and give the client the feeling of being understood and supported in his difficulties. However, what externally appears as friendliness and sincere love is in reality quite often nothing but manipulation and cold technical competence.

As the manuals describe it, the consultation process is supposed to be "collaborative" and to establish an interactive link, a "partnership" between the adviser and his client. Both are invited to full and active participation in the process of social change. The adviser draws out his or her client: making him "open up" and making bring out his confidences, "problems", "taboos", fears and inhibitions, anger, cultural or religious obstacles which prevent him from feeling "free" (in actual fact from becoming a slave of the new ethic). As for the client, he or she is pushed to commit to the "choices" toward which the adviser is guiding him or her and to become "responsible" for them. During this process, the adviser "clarifies" the client's values and the situation in which he finds himself. He helps him to establish priorities and to "take decisions". The adviser also teaches the client "negotiation" techniques for "safe" sexual relations.

The manuals describe the stages of the consultation process and provide typical expressions which the adviser can use at each stage. They explicitly mention the difficulties met with by advisers in getting their revolutionary message across and offer suggestions for overcoming them. They recommend that advisers be well versed in the culture in which they are operating, to stress its positive points, to listen to what the community have to say, to demonstrate "respect", to be "inclusive", to rely on the "objectivity" of science.

Education reform

Education reform is a theme of capital importance whose study goes beyond the scope of this manual. Since the 1960s and 1970s, generations have been educated at school of the "masters" of the western cultural revolution.

The family is the primary place for education of the conscience and human development, the privileged place for transmitting traditions and faith. When it does not fulfill its role, children, left to themselves and weakened, become easy to manipulate: they more easily allow themselves to be influenced by the surrounding culture, messages transmitted by music, provocative images, the media, youth groups, the ideas which go around and are taught at school and the social engineers' programs. As we have already said, the sexual revolution and the crisis in the family which it has brought about in the West have provoked a loss of personal and cultural identity which explains the speed and ease with which the new ideas have managed to impose themselves.

The global cultural revolution has fundamentally redefined the meaning of education. Its primary object is no longer the acquisition of *objective knowledge*, but the learning of *know-how* and *life skills*. Education now serves the acquisition, by all global citizens, of the agenda of the major UN conferences of the 1990s and their postmodern norms. To reach this goal, it is necessary, according to the expression once used by the former *United Nations University* rector Hans van Ginkel[6], to "redo education from within". The citizens of the world ought to learn to think and act *differently* – which is to say differently from their traditions.

The new "values" of education are now "good citizenship", exercising one's "rights", quality of life, protection from diseases such as AIDS, respect for the "rights of the future generations", individual autonomy, tolerance, social inclusion, good governance, *living together* (peace education), the celebration of diversity and multiculturalism, free choice of one's opinions, social role and identity, and sustainable development. Recognizing school as one of the principal forces of socialization, the agents of transformation have made it the privileged place for the transmission of these "values".

UNESCO, the UN agency which specializes in education, has developed "norms" supposed to orient the process of education reform at the global level. Recall that UNESCO is an intergovernmental agency which exerts direct influence on the education ministries of its member states. The agency has exerted effective pressure on these governments for them to re-evaluate and transform their curriculum contents, restructure their courses, and ensure that their teachers are themselves formed in the new global norms (*gender* in particular) – and this, from kindergarten to university.

Let us notice that the relation between UN organizations and national ministries is not subjected to direct democratic control: the object of their exchanges, though of critical importance for the society in question, is not openly debated at the national level. Let us further notice that the agents of change do not speak of *pressure* on governments, but of *support*: they pretend to *help* governments to honor their "commitments", while in reality they guide them surreptitiously toward the realization of their own agenda. Finally, let us note that in the domain of education reform as in that of health reform, the real partners of the UN are above all non-governmental (NGOs, federations of local authorities). The UN also relies on trade unions, such as *Education International*, whose membership includes millions of teachers throughout the world, and on *direct partnership* with teachers through the Internet[7], completely escaping control from the chain of authority.

"Life skills" and "quality" education

The current approach to development cooperation stipulates with good reason that there is no point taking children to school if they are poorly taught or if they leave after a few months. Education must be "quality". *Quality* is a key word in postmodern semantics. What does it mean?

Like the other concepts belonging to the postmodern ethic, *quality* is a "holistic" concept. So-called *quality education* includes reading, writing and numeracy, the acquisition of a good level of objective factual knowledge and general cultural knowledge verified by good exam results and other classical elements of education, together with the acquisition of what the new global language calls *life skills*. And what are *life skills*?

Life skills too are a badly defined holistic concept, including *inter alia*: "prevention", "knowledge of one's rights", "techniques for claiming them", good nutritional and hygienic habits, the acquisition of "tools" with which to "protect" oneself from the "risk" of "unwanted pregnancies" and sexually transmitted diseases (particularly AIDS), social and psychological techniques of contractual negotiation in "difficult" sexual relations. "Life skills" put the emphasis on the choice of the individual, and therefore on his responsibility for his own education. Within the framework of quality education, UNICEF wants to promote strong partnerships between the home, the school and the community in order to better coordinate strategies and access to condoms.

So-called *quality education* substantially transforms both the *content* of education, by integrating the above-mentioned elements, and the *process* of education. As a process, quality education insists on the student's *participation*, which is to say the participation of the student in transforming his own mentality. Let us repeat it: the child becomes a *direct partner* of the agents of cultural change.

According to the new ethic, the student is a *citizen* who, as such, is "equal" to the teacher. Quality education places on the same footing the *opinion* of the student and the *knowledge* or *authority* of the teacher. It constrains teachers to know, promote, respect and defend "children's rights". In the final analysis, the teacher no longer truly teaches. He becomes a *facilitator* helping students to exercise their rights, which is to say to *internalize* the new ethic. In the course of this process, the educator "learns" from his students: learning is reciprocal. The postmodern educational system abolishes hierarchies. It is horizontal.

The promoters of "life skills" insist on the pragmatic aspect of education, on learning by doing. They create a dialectical opposition between *knowledge* and *skill*. They say that traditional education, which used to be centered on *knowledge*, is abstract, external to the person and useless. On the other hand, "life skills based education" is, according to them, practical, internalized, owned by the student, and has direct practical usefulness. So-called *quality education* leads to a situation where the acquisition of "life skills" tends to be done to the *detriment* of education and of the acquisition of knowledge.

While the acquisition of knowledge is founded on criteria which are partly objective and universal, the acquisition of life skills depends on the *right to choose* exercised in a purely subjective manner. In the new postmodern culture, traditional education is seen as hierarchical, passive, sterile, top-down, authoritarian or fundamentalist – countercultural. Quality education, by contrast, is allegedly interactive, "participatory", practical, "democratic", directly useful: it is supposedly "bottom-up". It is supposed to develop the individual's capacity to "choose" and his personal responsibility. This development would be positive if it had not been hijacked. In practice, quality education *deconstructs* and *replaces* the teacher's legitimate authority with the student's *power* and *autonomy*. In a nutshell, education in the postmodern culture tends to reject the *in itself* to create a civilization where only the *for oneself* exists.

The agents of social transformation set themselves up as masters – as judges of what is, or is not, good and worthy to be taught. Their judgment is not submitted to the approval of states, schools, parents, or religious authorities. On the contrary, states, schools, parents and religions are supposed to conform to the global norms as the new educators interpret them.

The five stages of quality education

According to UNICEF, *quality education* comprises five stages or conditions.

1.- *Assessment.* The first stage of quality education consists in assessing the social and ethical baggage which the child brings to school and carries from his *early infancy.* Does the child come to school with an early infancy experience that is, for example, *gender sensitive?* In what ways do the language and values of his family differ from those of the new educators? What do the agents of social transformation deem necessary to correct in him?

2.- *Conducive environment.* The school environment where quality education takes place must be conducive to the transformation of mentalities: pleasant, "protective", "hygienic", "healthy", with water access. It must provide hygiene and health services, particularly reproductive and sexual health services. It must promote the physical and psycho-social-emotional health of both teachers and students. In brief, the environment in which quality education takes place should be *more* attractive than that of "ordinary" or traditional schools.

3.- *Transformation of the curriculum.* Quality education requires the school curriculum to be reformed, as we have seen, so as to include the acquisition of "life skills" and give priority care to girls' education.

4.- *"Democratic" education.* Teachers must use new teaching techniques, allegedly *child-centered,* meaning centered on the rights of children to express their opinions and to sexual and reproductive health. The teaching must promote children's participation in all aspects of school life.

5.- *Monitoring.* Finally, school results must be evaluated not only on the basis of the objective knowledge of the children, but also on their life skills and attitudes, their "positive participation" in society—this being judged in the light of national educational objectives, which are themselves created with the help of international organizations and their partners.

Quality education is circular: it starts and ends with an assessment made according to the criteria of the new ethic.

"Child-friendly" schools

UNICEF has conceived a new school model appropriate to the optimal realization of *quality education:* the so-called *child-friendly schools.*
Although the project currently rallies but a small proportion of schools,

child-friendly schools nevertheless reflect a major educational paradigm shift which has already taken on an unsuspected scope. *Child-friendly schools* allegedly respond to the needs of what UNICEF calls the *whole child*. They are concerned not only with the child's literacy, but also with his rights, health, nutrition and *general well-being*. Respect for children's rights contained in the *Convention on the Rights of the Child* is the founding principle of this new school model, but children's rights tend to be interpreted in a radical, postmodern light.

Although the new educational paradigm claims to be *holistic*, the fact is that the happiness of the child, his moral formation, his religious education - essential factors in education, are absent. Once again, postmodern "holism" turns out to be a reductionistic endeavor.

Child-friendly schools provide free and compulsory education. They forbid discrimination on the basis of any kind of "stereotype". They celebrate "diversity", in the sense in which the new ethic understands the concept, that is, including the "diversity of sexual orientations". They imperceptibly deconstruct the values that parental and religious education has given the child.

Child-friendly schools take into consideration the manner in which children are treated in their family and community, including times preceding and succeeding schooling. They are supposed to prove for all a "positive experience" and help parents, children and teachers to develop "harmonious relations". But do not these schools tend to develop an exclusive education model, which does not take into account the will of parents, families, individual cultures and religions?

Judging the tree by its fruit, should we not in conclusion question the utopian character of education which claims to be "quality", "life skills" and schools which are allegedly "child-friendly"? Have not the fruits of education reform since the end of the 1960s in fact been sexual promiscuity among young people, violence in schools, personality disorders, professional disorientation, lack of motivation and abyssal ignorance? It is now time for a serious, urgent and unescapable assessment of the results of education reform and the reliability of young people's knowledge.

Girls' education: acceleration campaigns

According to UNICEF, over 120 million children of school age are not benefiting from their fundamental right to education, and the majority of these are girls. International organizations have launched acceleration campaigns to enrol all girls in school and thereby ensure respect for their right to education as defined in the *Convention on the Rights of the Child* and the *Convention on the Elimination of All Forms of Discrimination against Women*. Recent UN policies, including those established at the *World Education Forum* (Dakar, 2000) and the *Millennium Development Goals*, have made the elimination of unequal *gender* access to primary and secondary school and compulsory primary education for all children major priorities of development cooperation until 2015.

UNICEF uses the words "Herculean" and "extraordinary" to describe the efforts undertaken to bring girls to school and "increase the quality of education", particularly in Africa, Asia and the Middle East. Some programs of the UN fund for children consist in seeking out girls who do not go to school, no matter how remote they are, bringing them to school and ensuring that they stay there until they have finished their schooling. To encourage girls' participation in school, the UN recommends placing schools closer to homes, multiplying them, lowering the cost of education, planning timetables to allow girls to carry out household tasks outside school hours, and recruiting women as teachers.

These international efforts in favor of girls' education, however, are not disinterested. They hide an agenda: they use girls' education to change the culture. Girls' education is not just about bringing girls to school, but about doing so to "empower" them, inculcate in them an awareness of their "rights", a sense of their "freedom to choose", their "autonomy" and "control" over their life and other values of the new postmodern ethic.

The real objective of girls' education is polyvalent: it combines women's economic and social "empowerment", increasing economic productivity, knowing the means to "protect" oneself from sexually transmitted diseases and "unwanted pregnancies", reducing the maternal and infant death rate, lowering the fertility rate (educated girls have fewer children because they marry later and are more likely to use contraception), stabilizing global population, improving the health and education prospects for future generations. We insist on the fact that girls' education does not include their individual development as persons, as if the woman essentially had to be at the service of global objectives which are, in addition, largely ideological.

The argument generally used to justify prioritizing girls is that their education contributes *more* to the health and education of the following generation than that of boys. We also note that the priority international cooperation gives to girls' education often ends up in policies and situations which discriminate against boys. It is not uncommon, in some areas, to find many more educated girls than educated boys.

Informal initiatives taken by the agents of social transformation on the ground

Outside the framework of formal education, the agents of the sexual revolution demonstrate an impressive determination, creativity and dynamism toward transforming mentalities, behaviors and lifestyles. Their field activity manuals provide numerous examples of the astonishing diversity of their initiatives. Here follow some examples.

LEISURE
- Creating youth centers offering recreational activities (games) and sexual education given by other young people (peer education).
- Drama productions, puppet shows, street theater, sketches relating their "experiences", "testimonies" followed by interactive discussions.
- Night cinema.
- Youth camps, sports activities, music, dance.
- Sale of materials for pleasure and relaxation.

MEDIA AND INTERNET:
- Television and radio programs.
- Newspaper articles written by young people for young people.
- Anonymous "counselling" services by telephone or email.
- Media campaigns, such as the BBC's sex education program Sexwise (70 million listeners).
- Internet sites, cybercafés, online services.

PUBLICITY CAMPAIGNS:
- Campaigns aimed at young people in schools and rural areas.
- Promoting a "positive image" of young people's sexuality through publicity.
- Mobile publicity working with local organizations in rural areas.

- Strategically placed posters in town.
- Distribution of gifts and souvenirs.
- Sensitization days on young people's sexual and reproductive health.
- National campaigns.
- Open letters.
- Celebration of international days (women's day, day against violence against women, AIDS day…).

MEETINGS:
- Community-level meetings.
- Home visits.
- Meetings of "satisfied clients".

SENSITIZATION, EDUCATION, TRAINING:
- Sensitization of religious leaders, seminarians, opinion-leaders, local authorities, educators, soldiers, university students, health workers…
- Training workshops for educators.
- Training young people in lobbying techniques.
- Speech training.
- Introduction of sex education into the school curriculum and activities.
- Developing detailed educational plans which include sexuality, sexual expression and sexual pleasure.
- Invitations to seminars for youth run by youth, sent to schools, youth organizations and the media.
- Training women to become catalysts and mobilizers in the community.
- Tests of knowledge levels and distribution of "national certificates" in the domain of reproductive health.
- Distributing information brochures.
- Public debates and conferences.
- Taking advantage of literacy programs to teach reproductive rights.
- Mobile conferences.
- Participatory educational methods.
- Volunteer training.
- Women's empowerment programs.
- Promoting the sexual rights of deaf, blind or disabled children in the name of the equality of all members of society.
- Collaboration with religious leaders, taking advantage of Friday sermons (Imams) or Sunday ones (Christian pastors).

- Forming wide networks of community facilitators to educate young people about claiming their sexual rights.
- Creation and reinforcement of youth clubs specialized in sexual and reproductive health, and creation of networks of youth groups.
- Collaboration with partner NGOs.
- Direct involvement of young people in planning and implementing reproductive health programs.
- Mobilizing families so that they can transform mentalities within their own family network.
- Creating programs linking young people with local and national decision-makers.
- Reinforcing youth centers and clinics which provide a complete range of services; increasing the choice of contraceptives, including the "morning after pill" for all young people.
- Creating networks of services including abortion.
- Partnerships with businesses and fund-raising.

The power of slogans

The agents of social transformation have demonstrated a genius for creating catchy slogans – lapidary, striking, dogmatic, dynamic, engaging, proactive, aggressive, comical… - which have been formidably effective in their success at rallying a critical mass of groups and individuals to their causes.

The slogans of the social engineers are manipulative and play on self-evident truths. They seem to propose a program to which nobody can be opposed, but they betray common sense and often hide an ideological or perverse agenda. When they shock, they do so in a seductive manner. The revolutionary fire which they often express is of a kind which generates enthusiasm. Here are a few examples, which we shall try to interpret briefly.

- *Every child must be a wanted child*: this dogmatic statement by Margaret Sanger seems to imply an altruistic, charitable and humanitarian attitude. The message it transmits is the following: we love children so much that, for their happiness, we wish to create a civilization where each of them is wanted and therefore loved. In reality, the slogan hides the selfishness of the man and the woman who are no longer disposed to gratuitous love and become the arbiters of the child's right to exist.

- *Brave and angry women*: the rallying cry of the IPPF from its beginnings, this slogan is comical. It evokes the "virtue" or the "merit" of women who have the courage to rebel against the "injustices" and disorders of this world. It gives radical feminists a heroic image.

- *Children by choice and not by chance*: the concept of choice evokes the power of the winning individual, his control over his destiny, while the word "chance" suggests the weakness of the losing individual, his poverty, incapacity and even irresponsibility.

- *Lust for life!*: this slogan used in campaigns against AIDS to promote the use of condoms is particularly perverse. It evokes the idea of sexual pleasure applied to the preservation of one's own life against illnesses and death. The message is: you can continue to have sex and celebrate pleasure in any context, as long as you use a condom.

- *Civil society is watching you*: a slogan invented by the eco-feminists to "keep an eye on governments" and pressure them to keep to their "commitments", which is to say in fact the program of radical NGOs. The message transmitted by this slogan is that NGOs are the guardians of ethics (the "good guys"), while governments and businesses have the tendency not to fulfill their responsibilities (the "bad guys").

- *Celebrating sexual diversity*: this slogan aims to transform into "cultural celebration" what is not yet totally accepted by the culture (the radical freedom to choose one's sexual orientation). It is a very effective way of deconstructing traditions. The agents of the sexual revolution want to be seen as on the side of festivity, community celebration, joy, and victory.

- *Times have changed*: this slogan takes advantage of the evidence that societies develop in the course of history, in order to gain acceptance for the idea that traditions should also "evolve", that certain values have become dated and that they should be got rid of if you want to be in keeping with your times.

- *Partnerships for a better world*: if you want to appear altruistic, on the side of solidarity, and participating in the world's humanitarian effort, you *must* engage in partnerships. The slogan omits to say that these partnerships often conceal a pre-established agenda and are oriented in a direction which will not make the world a better place.

- *From global to local*: this slogan exploits the common aspiration of mankind in favor of a return to the concrete, the local, the real. In fact it means the application at the local level of the norms (abstract, global, virtual) set up by minorities of experts working at the "global" level, at the UN and in its agencies.

- *No more speeches*: nobody wants any more "speeches" these days. The agents of change place themselves on the side of concrete active realization and implicitly place the "conservatives" on the side of rhetoric and inactivity. But what they want to apply is their own ideology, and not concrete development programs that people are waiting for.

- *From foes to partners*: this slogan aims to be reassuring. The social engineers display sincerity: they recognize that there have been confrontations and incompatibility between their views and certain groups in society (particularly businesses, cultures, traditions and religions). They announce a new approach: cooperation, partnership. Disagreements and confrontation are behind us. In reality the new approach consists in changing cultures and traditions from within to align them with the goals of the agents of transformation.

- *Vote for her life*: this slogan aims to salve the conscience of those who would vote in favor of laws allowing abortion or making "reproductive health" more accessible by giving them the impression that they are thereby carrying out an act of charity toward women.

- *All human rights for all*: the word "all" has a hidden trap in both cases. In its first usage, it means all human rights, including the new controversial rights studied in chapter four. In the second case, it is applied to "all", which is to say chiefly to minorities (homosexuals, lesbians, bisexuals, transgender, indigenous peoples, AIDS sufferers, immigrants, prostitutes, refugees, street children, the disabled and so on).

- *All different, all equal*: the idea conveyed by this slogan is practically the same as that of the previous one, but with the addition of "celebrating differences" within a framework which recognizes all value systems as radically equal.

- *Global problems require not only global solutions, but global values*: the agents of social transformation take the ethical high ground in global governance. They wish to justify, by what passes for self-evident truth, the necessity of "constructing" a new ethic. But they found their ethic on the "problems" of humanity, not on reality and the common good.

With no comment, let us mention the following other slogans:

- *Culture matters.*
- *Women's rights are human rights.*
- *Time is running out.*
- *Working from within and from without.*
- *Sexual rights, your everyday paradigm.*
- *Access equals life.*
- *Youth of the world, unite!*
- *A burning desire for change.*
- *Our survival is at stake.*
- *Let us celebrate our differences.*
- *Innovative alliances with the UN.*
- *Safe, legal and rare.*
- *Free to love safely.*
- *Make every mother and child count.*
- *I love you positive or negative.*
- *One is not born a woman, one becomes a woman.*

Change of strategy vis-à-vis cultures and religions: from confrontation to "collaboration"

The agents of transformation realized in the field that the real obstacles to the universal application of their ethical norms, and those of the Cairo and Beijing conferences in particular, were not technical but cultural and religious. They understood that if they did not succeed in bringing down these barriers, their project could fail.

Having conquered without difficulty, one after the other, most potential bastions of resistance (governments, businesses, international organizations other than the UN, educational systems, social services, "civil society", the media, all of which rapidly become, to varying degrees, their direct or indirect partners), the revolutionary agents still had to attack cultures, traditions and religions – their ultimate, and principal, challenge. Their strategy with regard to cultures and religions has changed radically[8]. It has shifted from direct confrontation, frontal attacks, aggression, to new forms of attack – subtle, indirect, difficult to perceive because taking place under the guise of a "friendly", "collaborative" and "partnership" approach. Henceforth the driving logic of partnerships is extended to everybody – not only to women, young people, men, governments, the media, NGOs, local authorities, businesses, but also to religious leaders – imams, rabbis and pastors. The realization of the Cairo and Beijing programs of action must be *everyone's business.*

The new strategy is manipulative. It attempts to demonstrate the "compatibility" of options that are incompatible by their very nature: cultural and religious traditions on the one hand, and the program of the global erotic revolution, on the other. The new strategy has abandoned the "negative" approach focusing on obstacles. It is ostensibly "positive": the agents of transformation exalt the social role of religions; they declare themselves to be "respectful of traditions". But their objective is to *transform* religious teaching and the behaviors of believers' *from within,* to align them with their own norms[9].

The social engineers have understood that changing cultures and religions *from within* was much more effective that attempting to impose their views *from without.* Advancing pragmatically wherever a favorable opening appears, taking care never to dilute their own objectives, they started using "soft" techniques to *neutralize* the resistance arising from religions. By striving to "understand each other better", they claim, it will be possible to overcome differences of "opinion". But, it should be noted, the teachings of the great religions are not a matter of "opinion".

The militants of the global erotic revolution recognize that their fight against cultural and religious traditions will require on their part courage, determination, audacity, tenacity and unbreakable perseverance, particularly in societies which they call "very conservative". The manuals[10] they are provided with encourage them to acknowledge all "progress", even when small, and to resist what they call the "false arguments" of religions, which is to say the arguments invoked to oppose the Cairo and Beijing agendas. The manuals recommend that agents of change devote time to studying the culture in which they operate to become familiar with the regional cultural tendencies, their "entry points" and their "obstacles", and thereby better target their programs.

The new "positive" strategy implies the adoption of a *participatory* and *inclusive* approach. The manuals recommend that social engineers consult people, listen to them, gather their views and desires, build trust with them, place community leaders on their side, and avoid all domineering behavior or remarks which could be perceived as judgment or criticism. Traditional or religious leaders are invited to engage themselves in the *mobilization* of their community and in transforming mentalities, and to leave the management of the "technical" aspects of these issues to sexual and reproductive health "professionals".

The agents of the global cultural revolution place the new ethical paradigms *above* religions. They believe that the function of religion is to provide a framework for human well-being and that, in as far as traditions stand in the way of the realization of sexual and reproductive health, they should be rejected without pity. They demand the examination of customs, cultures and religions in the light of the new rights, in order to make them achieve a balance and conform and adjust to the new conditions. Whatever opposes sexual and reproductive rights allegedly arises from "religious fundamentalism" and "irresponsibility". The new strategy surreptitiously integrates the right to choose and its radical derivatives into cultures and religious beliefs. It recommends that the agents of change strive to express these rights in a diversified way according to the specific nature of each culture. Sexual and reproductive rights are held to be *universal*, while cultures and religions would be *different* – which is to say devoid of universality.

The final objective of the new approach is to make people claim their sexual and reproductive "rights" in the name of the culture and religion they belong to. At the end of the revolutionary process, local populations should *appropriate to themselves* the new post-Judeo-Christian ethic and accept the new ways of thinking, above all those which call their beliefs into question. Each individual – woman, man, young person, child, disabled person, must "internalize" reproductive rights, making them so to speak their "everyday paradigm", and integrate them into the fabric of their life – *within* their own value system, without however changing culture or religion.

The agents of transformation present themselves as "rallying persons", "conflict managers", "mediators" who "do not judge" and stand "above all debate". Their principal mission is to "link" culture to human rights and give people the "power" to change cultural practices which they claim "violate" sexual and reproductive rights. Part of their propaganda is to present as "normal" or "natural" the tensions which arise in the course of the cultural transformation process, and not to deny the difficulties.

They even affirm that it is not possible to eliminate tensions completely, without by that token denying that it belongs to the logic of the *consensus process* to lead effectively to the resolution of conflicts existing within couples and local, national and "global" communities. For it is the mediators' role to *harmonize*, to unify cultures around their own values.

Proactive partnerships with religions

The agents of cultural transformation, having observed the preeminent effectiveness of partnerships with religious leaders and confessional NGOs, have decided to give strategic priority to reinforcing such partnerships. Monotheistic religions – with the Catholic Church in the first place by reason of its universal Magisterium – represent for them a major challenge. The authority of religions springs from divine revelation or at least from transcendence - hence the difficulty experienced by the revolutionary militants in deconstructing it. But this difficulty does not make them retreat. They are determined to *change* religions on certain points, not all at once or brutally, but little by little and subtly. It is religions which give them most problems, when their teachings oppose permissive "sex education" for adolescents, the use of condoms or contraception, abortion, homosexuality and other ideas and practices of the sexual revolution. The social engineers know that if they manage to destabilize religions on these points, their victory will be complete and definitive. What they want is to turn religions into "forces of chance", to make sexuality a dominant theme of religious discourse, from which they wish to eliminate all "taboos".

The strategy of the agents of transformation vis-à-vis religions is manifold:

- *"Diversity"*. The social engineers strategically insist on the *diversity* of viewpoints within a single religion in order to show that religions are not "monolithic" and that religious norms within a single religion are often interpreted, applied and practised *differently*. For example, the Holy See's position is held to represent but *one of the voices* of "Catholic orthodoxy": numerous are the Catholics who abort or practise contraception. It is thus possible, goes the propaganda, to be at once Catholic and for the "freedom to choose".

- *Support from "all religions" for the new ethic*. The social engineers also insist on the "fact" that religious leaders from all confessions support the Cairo and Beijing vision.

- *Contradiction between doctrine and practice.* They denounce the "flagrant contradictions" which they say exist between religious doctrines as they are taught and the real practices of the faithful.

- *Harmful effects and impediments to progress.* They organize awareness-raising campaigns on the "harmful effects" of certain cultural and religious practices. They "dialogue" on the way religions "hold up progress".

- *Redistribution of tasks.* They relegate to religions the role of compassion, and grant experts and NGOs the "technical" role. They push religious communities to engage in partnerships with entities "specialized" in sexual and reproductive health.

- *Balancing religions and the new ethic.* The approach of the agents of transformation allegedly consists in "balancing" religion and their own subversive objectives. They claim that they wish, not to destabilize religions in their foundations, but "only" to "adjust" them to the new ethic and to merely change the religious practices which, according to them, "violate" sexual and reproductive rights, while respecting other religious practices and the need of a society for "rituals".

- *Democratization of the religious discourse.* They attempt to "democratize" religious discourse by making women and young people "participate" in defining ethical norms, which all are supposed to implement.

- *Proactive attitude.* They put pressure on religious leaders to take the lead, speak to the faithful, and organize discussions on sexual and reproductive health in temples, mosques, synagogues, churches and other places of worship.

- *Perverse alliances.* The social engineers actively seek allies within communities of believers to turn them into what they call "progressive forces for change", in other words active partners of the new ideology, agents of change in their turn, who will introduce suspicion into consciences within their own communities.

- *Values clarification.* The agents of the revolution claim to know religions and cultures better than ordinary citizens and faithful, and propose to help them to "clarify" their values. In reality, what they "know" is ways of manipulating cultures and religions to redefine their content in the light of their own agenda. It is by "clarifying" what is correct from the standpoint of religion, what is legal, what is a universal human right, what is essential for health and so on that the enlightened despots of the new governance have hijacked the globalization process.

- *New theology*. They exhort religious leaders to develop what they call a "theology of compassion" and not of "judgment", and to find arguments in sacred texts and religious moral precepts which in fact support the social engineers' doctrine. They aim to transform the new postmodern ethic into a religious *duty*.

- *Horizontal process*. Unlike the cultural revolutions of the past, which took place vertically, cultural transformation is carried out *horizontally*, by *peers*. The horizontal mentality, fruit of the western cultural revolution and of the rejection of fatherhood and authority, implies, for example, that young people should commit to talking with their age mates about their sexual and reproductive rights, that "model governments" in the application of the new ethic encourage other governments to emulate them, that Catholics agreeing with the objectives of Cairo and Beijing commit to working at transforming the mentality of Catholics faithful to the Magisterium of the Church, that the South "helps" itself, and so on.

In reality, the horizontal process is a myth. The agents of transformation are *leaders in disguise*. They in effect govern the revolutionary process vertically. Besides, they call themselves *horizontal leaders*. Their will to govern and change society is beyond doubt. They proclaim themselves "above" religions. While they condemn all condemnation and all judgment, they set themselves up as judges of what favors the new ethic and condemn what goes against it. It is not rare to hear them say, for example in their campaigns promoting condoms or abortion "in good sanitary conditions", that it is necessary to "die to the moral authority of religions to save lives." Their goal is to reach a situation where believers call into question the teaching of their religion and swing to the side of the postmodern and post-Judeo-Christian ethic. They encourage these believers on the verge of apostasy , who practise what their religion condemns, to feel "good about themselves" and to remain proud of belonging to such or such religion.

KEY-WORDS OF THIS CHAPTER

Social transformation; quiet revolution; *from within*; social engineering; manipulation; informal process; propaganda; enabling; awareness-raising; agents of change; peer education; horizontal leader; consensus-building; values clarification; slogans; culturally sensitive approaches; negotiation process; quality education; life skills; appropriation; internalization; critical mass.

---

[1] Note the initiative of Bill Clinton entitled "The Power Within", which produces training programs supposed to motivate the general public and businesses: the organization of recreational events and conferences having, according to their own slogan, "the power to ignite your spirit" and allegedly enabling us to "learn from the-best-of-the-best real world experts who, in an incredibly entertaining environment, empower you to take action immediately and transform your life forever" (see www.powerwithin.com).

[2] The consensus process makes participants lose their "copyrights" over their specific contribution: the contribution of individual people is lost in the consensus and never attributed.

[3] The "indicators of progress" are elaborated by experts of UN agencies according to criteria that conform to their ideology. Governments are supposed to use these indicators to measure the "progress" they make in realizing the objectives of the great conferences and other objectives of the UN. The *Millennium Development Goals*, for example, are associated with 48 indicators at present. The UN's national teams have undertaken to create a common database whose statistics separate men and women (gender disaggregated data).

[4] We cite the example of the UNDP which in 2003 published a manual on "Drafting gender-aware legislation". This manual is written for the attention of lawyers and politicians. It guides the drafting of laws which integrate the "gender perspective", in a practical and differentiated way, according to the central and eastern regions of Europe and the CIS.

[5] UNICEF educates countries through "capacity-building" programs. The UN begins by evaluating the situation of children in the country, identifying the role played by *gender* in education. The UN agencies and the government then prepare a common evaluation of the country ("Common Country Assessment") which constitutes an important stage in formulating a new cooperation program. Then the UN develops a "Development Assistance Framework".

[6] See IIS Report 191. Johannesburg Summit. The Education Revolution. Marguerite A. Peeters. 2002.

[7] UNESCO has produced, for example, an Internet site and a CD for teachers on sustainable development education; it contains a hundred hours of distance learning courses, free and independent of schools' authority and that of national education ministers. The agency believes that it can reach directly sixty million teachers in this way.

[8] The new strategy was the theme of a conference in Amsterdam in 2004, organized by UNFPA on the occasion of the tenth anniversary of the Cairo conference. At this conference on "partnership with cultures and religions", for the first time the relation between sexual and reproductive rights on the one hand and cultures and religions on the other was broadly addressed – a subject which until then had remained taboo.

[9] UNFPA explains that it is a matter of "acting from within" "culturally sensitive contexts" (in other words cultures which resist subversive objectives) to "implant" in them the Cairo and Beijing programs.

[10] See for example UNFPA. Culture Matters. Working with Communities and Faith-based Organizations: Case Studies from Country Programmes. 2004.

Conclusion

The challenges of postmodern civilization are those of the end of a world: the end of modernity and consequently the end of the vision which has inspired culture for such a long time, the end of history, the end of ideologies, the end of representative democracy, the end of politics and of left and right wing political parties, the end of social hierarchies, the end of the American Anglo-Protestant creed[1], the end of the Atlantic alliance, the end of philosophy, the end of the West.

The revolutions whose radical aspects we have studied in this manual have also produced positive cultural changes, deserving study and serious consideration in their own right. They have had the effect, for example, of disengaging western and particularly European culture from ready-made ideas, stereotypes and other sterile and abstract constructions. Machismo, moralism, dogmatism, paternalism, feminism, elitism, institutionalism, intellectualism, formalism, pharisaism, absolutism, western cultural imperialism, rationalism, with all their burden of abstraction, lack of personal commitment and love, are dying.

But while the emerging global civilization is called to be that of love, the postmodern paradigms which are already replacing the paradigms of modernity – such as consensus, appropriation, participatory democracy, holism, freedom of choice, gender equality, the non-repressive civilization... - are vitiated by radicalism and hijack what men and women living at the start of the third millennium really desire.

Dismantling the system of the new global ethic piece by piece is a Sisyphean and probably impossible endeavor. By contradistinction, it is possible to actively propose to humanity a positive alternative. Love and truth, charity, friendly synergy among the members of the social body, sincere and active participation of each person in the life of society, integral humanism developing the person in his completeness and thus open to his eternal predestination, fraternal openness to all cultures, self-determination and personal commitment, authentic freedom, and seeking the happiness of all: isn't this the platform of those who want to seize the opportunities of the times we live in, conform to its duties and commit themselves in the way of a new leadership?

Such opportunities in fact do exist. Even as it seems to have won over to its secularist agenda the majority of actors in global governance, the new global ethic has already revealed by its fruits the utopianism of its propositions. The constructions of postmodern radicalism, resting as we have seen on shifting sands, could collapse in the same way, and probably much more rapidly, in which the Berlin wall came down – as a result of a quiet self-destruction.

The time has come to start working with courage and zeal to bring about a return, not to the sociopolitical structures of the past, but to the original design of the Creator. We are called to choose freely whom we want to be, to declare ourselves autonomous from the system of the "new global ethic", to practise charity, to be active, to exercise our responsibilities, to decide to be ourselves.

[1] See Samuel Huntington's book "Who are we?". Free Press. 2004.

References

en.wikiquote.org/wiki/Alfred_Kinsey

en.wikiquote.org/wiki/shulamith_firestone

European Commission. 2004. *Toolkit on mainstreaming gender equality in EC development cooperation.*

European Communities. 2006. *The European consensus for development.*

European Parliament. 2003. *Final Report on the proposal for a decision of the EP and of the Council establishing a Community action programme to promote organizations active at European level in the field of equality between men and women.*

IPPF. 1996. *Guidelines for the use of the IPPF Charter on Sexual and Reproductive Rights.* Edited by Karen Newman.

IPPF. 1996. IPPF Charter on Sexual and Reproductive Rights.

IPPF. 2002. *Programme guidance on counseling for STI/HIV prevention in sexual and reproductive health settings. For counselors, health workers, educators and all those working in STI/HIV/AIDS.* www.ippf.org

IPPF. 1992. *Vision 2000. Strategic Plan.*

IPPF. 1998. *Youth manifesto.* www.ippf.org

Marcuse, Herbert. 1962. *Eros and Civilization.* Vintage Edition.

NSSM 200

Peeters, Marguerite. 2001. *Hijacking Democracy. The Power Shift to the Unelected.* www.aei.org

Peeters, Marguerite. 2003. *Participatory Democracy in the New Europe: a Critical Analysis.* www.aei.org

Peeters, Marguerite. 1995-2008. *Reports 1-275.* Interactive Information Services.

Peeters, Marguerite. 2006. *The New Global Ethic: Challenges for the Church.* Institute for Intercultural Dialogue Dynamics.

Peeters, Paul. 1974. *Herbert Marcuse : Eros and Civilization.*

Petchesky, Rosalind P. 2000. *Reproductive and Sexual Rights.* United Nations Research Institute for Social Development. Occasional Paper 8.

Rorty, Richard. 1982. *Consequences of Pragmatism.* University of Minnesota Press.

Rorty, Richard. 1989. *Contingency, Irony, and Solidarity.* Cambridge University Press.

seattle.wa.lwv.org/pubs/womhist2002.pdf

Singh, Jyoti Shankar. 1998. *Creating a New Consensus on Population.* Earthscan Publications. London.

UNDP. 2003. *Human Development Report.*

UNDP. 2003. *Millennium Development Goals. National Reports. A Look through a Gender Lens.*

UNESCO. 2000. *Gender Sensitivity.* Module 5.

UNESCO. 2002. *UNESCO Universal Declaration on Cultural Diversity.*

UNFPA. 2001. *Application of Human Rights to Reproductive and Sexual Health.* Recommendations.

UNFPA. 2004. *Culture Matters. Working with Communities and Faith-based Organizations : Case Studies from Country Programmes.*

UNFPA. 2005. *Guide pour Agir de l'Intérieur. 24 Conseils pour Implanter un Programme dans un Contexte Culturel Sensible.*

UNFPA. 2001. *Reproductive Health Commodity Security: Partnerships for Change. The UNFPA Strategy.*

UNFPA. 2005. *State of the World Population 2005: Gender Equity, Reproductive Health and the Millennium Development Goals.*

UNFPA. 2005. *State of the World Population.* Press release.

UNFPA. 1999. *The Right to Choose. Reproductive Rights and Reproductive Health.*

UN General Assembly. 2000. *Further actions and initiatives to implement the Beijing Declaration and Platform for Action.* Resolution A/RES/ S-23/3.

UN General Assembly. 2003. *Integrated and coordinated implementation of and follow-up to the outcomes of the major United Nations conferences and summits in the economic and social fields.* Resolution *A/RES/57/270B.*

UN General Assembly. 2000. *Political Declaration.* Resolution A/RES/S-23/2.

UNIFEM. 2002. *Progress of the world's women. Gender equality and the Millennium Development Goals.* UNIFEM biennial report.

UN Secretary General. 2003. *Follow-up to and progress in the implementation of the Beijing Declaration and Platform for Action and the outcome of the twenty-third special session.* Report A/58/166.

Whelan, Robert. 1992. *Whose Choice: Population Controllers' or yours?* Committee on Population and the Economy. London.

WHO. 2002. *Integrating Gender Perspectives in the Work of WHO.*

WHO. 2004. *Reproductive Health: draft strategy to accelerate progress towards the attainment of international goals and targets.* WHA57.12.

WHO. 2004. *Reproductive Health.* Report by the Secretariat. A57/13.

WHO. 2003. *Safe Abortion: Technical and Policy Guidance for Health Systems.*

womenshistory.about.com/library/qu/blqusang.htm

World Bank. 2003. *Gender Equality and the Millennium Development Goals.* Gender and Development Group.

www.marxists.org/reference/archive/marcuse/works/eros-civilisation/intro-duction.htm

www.powerwithin.com

www.wikipedia.org/Wiki/Metrosexual.

ANNEX A

KEY-WORDS AND EXPRESSIONS
OF THE GLOBAL FEMINIST AND SEXUAL REVOLUTION

Acceleration	Gender disaggregated data	Partners, partnership
Access	Gender discrimination	Peer education
Action, actor	Gender disparity	People-centered
Agenda, agent of change	Gender equality	Postmodernity
Attitude	Gender equity	Prevention
Awareness-raising	Gender gap	Primary health care
Behavior change	Gender mainstreaming	Process of change
Bodily integrity	Gender neutral	Quality of life
Best practices	Gender norms	Reproductive and sexual health and rights
Capacity-building	Gender stereotype	Responsible
Civil society	Gender violence	Right to choose
Commitment	Global ethic	Safe
Conducive environment	Globalization	Sensitization
Consciousness	Governance	Social contract
Consensus	Harmful practices	Social engineering
Constructivist	Holism	Social justice
Control of one's life	Imbibe	Social transformation
Couple	Implementation	Stereotype
Cross-cutting	Indicator of progress	Sustainable development
Cultural diversity	Individual	Systemic
Culturally sensitive approaches	Internalize	Targets
Deconstruction	Life skills	Tolerance
Education	Lifestyle	Training
Empowerment	Linkage	Transnational
Enabling environment	Mainstreaming	Unmet need
Expert, expertise	Monitor	Unwanted pregnancy
Facilitator	Multistakeholder	Vision
Family under all its forms	NGOs	Watchdog
For all	Norm, norm-setting	Well-being
Gender	Owner, ownership	Win-win
Gender contract	Participation, participatory democracy	

ANNEX B

MAIN ACTORS AND PARTNERS
OF THE REVOLUTION

We do not subscribe to a *conspiracy theory*, which would presuppose a duly considered strategic plan to grab global power on the part of a minority of identifiable "conspirators". Rather, we consider the current global cultural deconstruction to be the endogenous fruit of a long and complex secularization process. We consider, on the one hand, that *witch hunts* are simplistic and counterproductive, and on the other that history does go through man and that the history of the revolution is that of the men and women who have enacted it down the generations. The following module gives us a glimpse of the individuals, institutions and historical developments which played a particularly critical role in this long process of deconstruction, without one being able to say of any of them that they had a birds-eye view of the revolution's scope and its long-term consequences on societies.

- The *spearhead individuals*: militant and often charismatic leaders of the revolutionary movement, these individuals or groups, who are a minority, propose a striking vision. They express it through slogans, books or speeches and generate *mass movements*, institutes or NGOs to promote it.

- The *followers*: fertile ground for subversive ideas, these individuals belong to the entourage of the "spearheads", become their disciples and propagate the new ideas. Once the revolution has acquired a critical momentum, its agents organize themselves into *networks* of *partners*.

- The *unconscious and manipulated majority*: as the base of the revolution broadens, the majority gradually lets itself be seduced and begins to compromise. It ends up losing its own values and swinging to the side of the revolution. Social engineering techniques allow the agents of transformation to co-opt even those who would resist them if they were properly informed and educated.

- *Institutional vectors*: under constant pressure from the minorities, and faced with the majority's passivity, institutions internalize the revolution's ideas and transform them into social norms applicable to all.

At the end of the revolutionary process, the partners are *legion*. *Scientists* have given their ideological objectives a scientific justification and developed technologies for realizing them. Economic and commercial interests (pharmaceutical firms, cinema, music, Internet...) have grafted themselves onto the revolution. Foundations and businesses finance it. Pundits and philosophers have justified it by "rational" motives and have given it an intellectual foundation. Schools and universities teach its ideas to the young generation. International organizations have transformed it into a global consensus. Local authorities propagate it at the local level. Governments base laws and national policies on it. Trades unions transform its gains into social rights to be claimed.

"SPEARHEAD" FEMINISTS

1869-1940	Emma Goldman
1879-1966	Margaret Sanger
1880-1958	Marie Stopes
1908-1986	Simone de Beauvoir
1920-1998	Bella Abzug
1921-	Betty Friedan
1923-	Kate Millett
1934-	Gloria Steinem
1935-	Susan Brownmiller
1937-	Jane Fonda
1943-	Frances Kissling
1945-	Shulamith Firestone...

SCIENTISTS

1766-1834	Thomas Robert Malthus, economist
1809-1882	Charles Darwin, naturalist
1903-1967	Gregory Pincus, doctor
1894-1956	Alfred Kinsey, sexologist
1926-	Etienne Emile Beaulieu, doctor
1932-	Paul R. Erhlich, biologist...

COMMERCIAL DEVELOPMENTS

20th century	Development of the cinema
1950-60	Commercialization of television
1960	Commercialization of contraception
1988	Commercialization of RU486
1995	Commercialization of the Internet...

INFLUENTIAL BOOKS

1848	The Communist Manifesto (Marx and Engels)
1884	The Origin of the Family, Private Property and the State (Engels)
1922	The Pivot of Civilization (Sanger)
1929	Civilization and its Discontents (Freud)

1948	Sexual Behavior in the Human Male (Kinsey)
1949	The Second Sex (de Beauvoir)
1955	Eros and Civilization (Marcuse)
1966	The Order of Things (Foucault)
1968	The Population Bomb (Ehrlich)
1970	Sexual Politics (Millett)
1972	The Limits to Growth (Meadows)
1979	The Dialectic of Sex (Firestone)…

PHILOSOPHERS AND THINKERS

1711-1776	David Hume
1712-1778	Jean-Jacques Rousseau
1724-1804	Emmanuel Kant
1768-1834	Friedrich Schleiermacher
1770-1831	Friedrich Hegel
1775-1833	Ludwig Feuerbach
1788-1860	Arthur Schopenhauer
1813-1855	Soren Kierkegaard
1818-1883	Karl Marx
1820-1895	Friedrich Engels
1822-1911	Francis Galton
1844-1900	Frederic Nietzsche
1856-1939	Sigmund Freud
1889-1951	Ludwig Wittgenstein
1889-1976	Martin Heidegger
1891-1937	Antonio Gramsci
1898-1979	Herbert Marcuse
1905-1980	Jean-Paul Sartre
1924-1998	Jean-François Lyotard
1926-1984	Michel Foucault
1929-	Jürgen Habermas
1930-2004	Jacques Derrida
1931-	Richard Rorty
1959-	Michel Onfray…

THE GENERATION AT THE RUDDER OF GLOBAL GOVERNANCE IN 1990 AND INDIVIDUAL POLITICAL PERSONALITIES

- Willy Brandt
- Halfdan Mahler
- Maurice Strong
- Gro Harlem Brundtland
-Tim Wirth
- Carol Bellamy

- Bill Clinton
- Hillary Clinton
- Al Gore
- Richard Jolly
- Gustave Speth
- Nafis Sadik
- Fred Sai
- Ingar Brueggeman
- Steven Sinding
- Thoraya Obaid
- Mary Robinson
- Ted Turner
- Louis Michel…

FOUNDATIONS
- Buffett Foundation
- Carnegie Foundation
- Ford Foundation
- Bill & Melinda Gates Foundation
- William and Flora Hewlett Foundation
- John D. and Catherine T. MacArthur Foundation
- David and Lucile Packard Foundation
- Rockefeller Foundation
- Rutgers Foundation
- Soros
- UN Foundation...

NGOS AND HUMANITARIAN ORGANIZATIONS
- IPPF and its member associations
- IUSSP
- Marie Stopes International
- Earth Council
- Amnesty International
- Astra Network
- Care International
- Catholics for a Free Choice
- Center for Reproductive Law and Policy
- Center for Development and Population Activities (CEPDA)
- Center for Population Options
- Church World Service
- Commonwealth Medical Association
- Family Health International
- Global Health Council

- Humane Society of America
- Human Rights Watch
- International Lesbian and Gay Association
- International Women's Health Coalition
- Ipas
- European Women's Lobby
- National Abortion Federation
- National Abortion Rights Action League
- Pathfinder International
- Population Crisis Committee
- Population Institute / Population Action Council
- Population Reference Bureau
- Save the Children
- Sierra Club
- Women's Environment and Development Organization (WEDO)
- Green Cross International
- Parliamentarians for Global Action
- Population Action International
- Greenpeace
- WWF
- Human Rights Watch
- State of the World Forum
- Amnesty International
- Friends of the Earth
- Oxfam
- Various informal lobbies...

POLITICAL PARTIES
At the outset:
- The Socialist International and socialists
- The Green parties
- US Democrats

Later:
- Christian Democrats
- US Republicans...

PARLIAMENTARIANS
- Parliamentarians for Global Action
- European Parliamentary Forum for Population and Development
- African and Arab Parliamentarians' Forum for Population and Development
- Interamerican Parliamentary Group for Population and Development
- Asian Parliamentarians' Forum for Population and Development...

ACADEME AND THINK TANKS
- Center for African Family Studies
- Center for Population and Family Health, Columbia University
- Global Reproductive Health Forum, Harvard University
- Guttmacher Institute
- Harvard School of Public Health's François-Xavier Bagnoud Center for Health and Human Rights
- Hunter College
- Institute for Reproductive Health, Georgetown University
- Institute for Research on Women and Gender, Columbia University
- Johns Hopkins School of Public Health
- Office of Population Research, Princeton University
- Population Council
- Population Institute
- Women's Health Project at the University of the Witwatersrand
- World Resources Institute...

CLUBS AND PARALLEL NETWORKS
- The Club of Rome
- Clinton's Global Initiative
- The Power Within…

UN BODIES
- UNFPA
- WHO
- UNICEF
- UNAIDS
- UNDP and its resident coordinators
- ECOSOC
- UN FUND FOR INTERNATIONAL PARTNERSHIPS
- Secretariat (DESA, OSAGI)
- Regional Commissions (Economic Commission for Africa, Economic and Social Commission for Asia and the Pacific…)
- UN Women
- World Bank…

INTERNATIONAL AND SUPRANATIONAL INSTITUTIONS
- European Commission and its Development DG
- G-8
- OECD
- NATO
- NEPAD

- The Commonwealth
- Francophonie…

GOVERNMENTS WHICH ARE PARTICULARLY IMPLICATED
- United Kingdom
- Netherlands
- Scandinavian countries: Norway, Sweden, Denmark
- Japan
- United States…

NATIONAL MINISTRIES
- Foreign Affairs (in North America: Secretary of State, USAID)
- Culture
- Development / Cooperation
- Sustainable Development
- Economics and Finance
- Education
- Environment
- Women or Gender
- Youth
- Planning
- Health…

BUSINESSES AND HIGH FINANCE
- International Chamber of Commerce
- The Global Compact, and member companies
- World Business Council for Sustainable Development
- Pharmaceuticals, cosmetics, film and advertising companies, theaters, the entertainment industry
- World Economic Forum
- Goldman Sachs…

RELIGIONS
- World Council of Churches
- Temple of Understanding
- United Religions Initiative
- Parliament of the World's Religions
- Cathedral of Saint John the Divine
- Traditional religions (chiefdoms…)
- Partners *within* the great religions…

LOCAL AUTHORITIES
International Union of Local Authorities and its millions of members...

TRADE UNIONS
Education International...

YOUTH
- Global Youth Partners
- Global Youth Coalition
- Youth Parliament
- Children's Parliament...

ANNEX C

THE POST-COLD WAR CONFERENCE PROCESS
OF THE UNITED NATIONS

Year	Location	Theme	"Gain"
1990	Jomtien	Education for all	"For all"
1990	New-York	Children	Children's rights
1992	Rio	Environment	Sustainable development
1993	Vienna	Human rights	Rights culture
1994	Cairo	Population	Reproductive health
1995	Copenhagen	Social development	New social contract
1995	Beijing	Women	Gender perspective
1996	Istanbul	Habitat	Partnership principle
1996	Rome	Food security	Holism
2001	Brussels	Least developed countries	
2001	New-York	AIDS	
2001	Durban	Racism	
2002	Monterrey	Development finance	
2002	Madrid	Aging	
2003	Geneva	Telecommunications	

Follow-up conferences

Year	Location	Theme	
1996	Amman	Jomtien + 5	
1997	New York	Rio + 5	
1999	New York	Cairo + 5	
2000	Genève	Copenhagen + 5	
2000	New York	Beijing + 5	
2000	Dakar	Jomtien + 10	
2001	New York	Istanbul + 5	
2002	Johannesburg	Rio + 10	
2002	New York	New York + 10	
2004	Amsterdam	Cairo + 10	
2005	New York	Beijing + 10	

Important previous conferences

Year	Location	Theme	
1968	Tehran	Human rights	
1972	Stockholm	Environment	
1974	Bucharest	Population	
1975	Mexico	Women	
1980	Copenhagen	Women	
1984	Mexico	population	
1985	Nairobi	Women	

ANNEX D

OTHER IMPORTANT EVENTS

1968 Western revolt of the youth
1978 Paradigm of *Health for all* through *primary health care* (Alma Ata)
1979 Convention on the Elimination of All Forms of Discrimination against Women
1986 Right to Development
1987 Brundtland Report on *Sustainable Development*
1990 Convention on the Rights of the Child
1991 Report of the Stockholm high-level strategic meeting on global governance: *Common Responsibility in the 1990's*
1992 Framework Convention on Climate Change
1993 Creation of the High Commission for Human Rights
1993 *Universal Declaration of a Global Ethic* (Parliament of the World's Religions)
1995 Report of the Global Commission for Culture and Development: *Our Creative Diversity*
1997 First mandate of Kofi Annan. Reform of the UN
1997 Framework project of *Universal Ethics* (UNESCO)
1997 Kyoto Protocol
1998 World Conference of ministers Responsible for Youth (Lisbon)
1998 Creation of the International Criminal Court (Rome)
1998 Nomination of Gro Harlem Brundtland to WHO. WHO reform New policy of Health for All
1998 First anti-globalization demonstration at Seattle
1999 Preparatory meeting at Cairo plus five (The Hague)
1999 Launch of the Global Compact with Businesses (Davos)
1999 Nomination of Koichiro Matsuura to UNESCO
2000 Final version of the *Earth Charter* (Paris)
2000 Millennium Summit and *Millennium Declaration* (New York)
2001 Second mandate of Kofi Annnan
2001 Nomination of Thorava Obaid to UNFPA
2001 Events of September 11
2002 *Universal Declaration on Cultural Diversity* (UNESCO)
2004 Reports of two High Level Committees: UN and civil society, and security
2005 Summit in New York for the sixtieth anniversary of the UN and reform plan
2006 Nomination of Ban Ki-moon as Secretary General of the UN
2006 Report of the High Level Committee on the coherence of the UN system

ANNEX E

DEMOCRATIC PROCESS VS. "CONSENSUAL" PROCESS

The table below identifies some of the main differences between the traditional democratic process and the consensus process. It helps apprehend the nature of the challenges posed by the new political culture in which we are now.

Democratic process	"Consensual" process
Majority – opposition	Equal participants
Debate	Negotiations
Majority vote	Elimination of differences
Clear identities	Compromises
Win – lose	Win – win
Hierarchical leadership	Horizontal leadership
Decision-makers' responsibility	Usurpation of influence
Representation	Participation
Authentic pluralism	Relativism
Transparency	Manipulation
Common good and truth	Consensus as a value in itself
Service	Sum of particular interests
Formal	Informal
Competition	Convergence

For more information

The Institute for Intercultural Dialogue Dynamics studies the key concepts, values and operational mechanisms of globalization.

The Institute produces in-depth analytical reports on these topics and monitors developments at the multilateral and global levels. The Institute also produces didactic materials destined to a wider audience, such as manuals, modules, training kits and slides, and regularly updates a lexicon of the key words of the global ethic. The Institute participates in and organizes conferences, round-tables, awareness-raising seminars and training-of-trainers seminars. It occasionally makes policy prescriptions.

After having painstakingly identified the radical components of global cultural change, the Institute increasingly focuses on exploring the concrete possibilities for a positive alternative responding to the real aspirations of contemporary men and women.

The Institute's approach is interactive. We are happy to receive your questions, comments, criticisms, suggestions and contributions and to respond to them to the extent of our possibilities.

Contact :
admin@dialoguedynamics.com

www.ingramcontent.com/pod-product-compliance
Lightning Source LLC
Chambersburg PA
CBHW070035100426
42740CB00013B/2700